T0384913

An Analysis of

Roland Barthes's

Mythologies

John M. Gómez

Published by Macat International Ltd
24:13 Coda Centre, 189 Munster Road, London SW6 6AW.

Distributed exclusively by Routledge
2 Park Square, Milton Park, Abingdon, Oxon OX14 4RN
711 Third Avenue, New York, NY 10017, USA

Routledge is an imprint of the Taylor & Francis Group, an informa business

www.macat.com
info@macat.com

Cataloguing in Publication Data
A catalogue record for this book is available from the British Library.
Library of Congress Cataloguing-in-Publication Data is available upon request.
Cover illustration: Etienne Gilfillan

ISBN 978-1-912302-81-9 (hardback)
ISBN 978-1-912127-96-2 (paperback)
ISBN 978-1-912281-69-5 (e-book)

Notice
The information in this book is designed to orientate readers of the work under analysis,
to elucidate and contextualise its key ideas and themes, and to aid in the development
of critical thinking skills. It is not meant to be used, nor should it be used, as a
substitute for original thinking or in place of original writing or research. References and
notes are provided for informational purposes and their presence does not constitute
endorsement of the information or opinions therein. This book is presented solely for
educational purposes. It is sold on the understanding that the publisher is not engaged
to provide any scholarly advice. The publisher has made every effort to ensure that
this book is accurate and up-to-date, but makes no warranties or representations with
regard to the completeness or reliability of the information it contains. The information
and the opinions provided herein are not guaranteed or warranted to produce particular
results and may not be suitable for students of every ability. The publisher shall not be
liable for any loss, damage or disruption arising from any errors or omissions, or from
the use of this book, including, but not limited to, special, incidental, consequential or
other damages caused, or alleged to have been caused, directly or indirectly, by the
information contained within.

CONTENTS

THE MACAT LIBRARY

The Macat Library is a series of unique academic explorations of seminal works in the humanities and social sciences – books and papers that have had a significant and widely recognised impact on their disciplines. It has been created to serve as much more than just a summary of what lies between the covers of a great book. It illuminates and explores the influences on, ideas of, and impact of that book. Our goal is to offer a learning resource that encourages critical thinking and fosters a better, deeper understanding of important ideas.

Each publication is divided into three Sections: Influences, Ideas, and Impact. Each Section has four Modules. These explore every important facet of the work, and the responses to it.

This Section-Module structure makes a Macat Library book easy to use, but it has another important feature. Because each Macat book is written to the same format, it is possible (and encouraged!) to cross-reference multiple Macat books along the same lines of inquiry or research. This allows the reader to open up interesting interdisciplinary pathways.

To further aid your reading, lists of glossary terms and people mentioned are included at the end of this book (these are indicated by an asterisk [*] throughout) – as well as a list of works cited.

Macat has worked with the University of Cambridge to identify the elements of critical thinking and understand the ways in which six different skills combine to enable effective thinking.
Three allow us to fully understand a problem; three more give us the tools to solve it. Together, these six skills make up the **PACIER** model of critical thinking. They are:

ANALYSIS – understanding how an argument is built
EVALUATION – exploring the strengths and weaknesses of an argument
INTERPRETATION – understanding issues of meaning

CREATIVE THINKING – coming up with new ideas and fresh connections
PROBLEM-SOLVING – producing strong solutions
REASONING – creating strong arguments

To find out more, visit **WWW.MACAT.COM.**

CRITICAL THINKING AND *MYTHOLOGIES*

Primary critical thinking skill: ANALYSIS
Secondary critical thinking skill: CREATIVE THINKING

Roland Barthes's 1957 *Mythologies* is a masterpiece of analysis and inter-pretation. At its heart, Barthes's collection of essays about the "mythologies" of modern life treats everyday objects and ideas – from professional wrestling, to the Tour de France, to Greta Garbo's face – as though they are silently putting forward arguments. Those arguments are for modernity itself, the way the world is, from its class structures, to its ideologies, to its customs.

In Barthes's view, the mythologies of the modern world all tend towards one aim: making us think that the way things are, the status quo, is how they should naturally be. For Barthes, this should not be taken for granted; instead, he suggests, it is a kind of mystification, preventing us from seeing things differently or believing they might be otherwise. His analyses do what all good analytical thinking does: he unpicks the features of the arguments silently presented by his subjects, reveals their (and our) implicit assumptions, and shows how they point us towards certain ideas and conclusions. Indeed, understanding Barthes' methods of analysis means you might never see the world in the same way again.

ABOUT THE AUTHOR OF THE ORIGINAL WORK

Born in France in 1915, **Roland Barthes** was one of the major observers and theorists of culture of the twentieth century. He is best known for his analyses of French culture, his literary criticism, and his contributions to photography theory. Barthes's work is considered revolutionary for the way it looked at popular culture from a serious, academic perspective. He died, rather unfortunately, in 1980 at the age of 64 after being hit by a laundry van while walking in Paris.

ABOUT THE AUTHOR OF THE ANALYSIS

Dr John M. Gómez was awarded his PhD by the University of Cambridge for a thesis on recorded music, literature and modernity from 1914 to 1955. He now travels widely to DJ Brazilian jazz, and divides the remainder of his time between homes in London and Madrid.

ABOUT MACAT

GREAT WORKS FOR CRITICAL THINKING

Macat is focused on making the ideas of the world's great thinkers accessible and comprehensible to everybody, everywhere, in ways that promote the development of enhanced critical thinking skills.

It works with leading academics from the world's top universities to produce new analyses that focus on the ideas and the impact of the most influential works ever written across a wide variety of academic disciplines. Each of the works that sit at the heart of its growing library is an enduring example of great thinking. But by setting them in context – and looking at the influences that shaped their authors, as well as the responses they provoked – Macat encourages readers to look at these classics and game-changers with fresh eyes. Readers learn to think, engage and challenge their ideas, rather than simply accepting them.

'Macat offers an amazing first-of-its-kind tool for interdisciplinary learning and research. Its focus on works that transformed their disciplines and its rigorous approach, drawing on the world's leading experts and educational institutions, opens up a world-class education to anyone.'

Andreas Schleicher
Director for Education and Skills, Organisation for Economic Co-operation and Development

'Macat is taking on some of the major challenges in university education ... They have drawn together a strong team of active academics who are producing teaching materials that are novel in the breadth of their approach.'

Prof Lord Broers,
former Vice-Chancellor of the University of Cambridge

'The Macat vision is exceptionally exciting. It focuses upon new modes of learning which analyse and explain seminal texts which have profoundly influenced world thinking and so social and economic development. It promotes the kind of critical thinking which is essential for any society and economy.
This is the learning of the future.'

Rt Hon Charles Clarke, former UK Secretary of State for Education

'The Macat analyses provide immediate access to the critical conversation surrounding the books that have shaped their respective discipline, which will make them an invaluable resource to all of those, students and teachers, working in the field.'

Professor William Tronzo, University of California at San Diego

WAYS IN TO THE TEXT

KEY POINTS

- Roland Barthes is among the most important theorists of culture of the twentieth century.

- Published in 1957, *Mythologies* argues that it is possible to read everyday objects and activities as being charged with ideological* meaning—that is, roughly, as representing and endorsing certain political and social ideas of how the world is and should be.

- *Mythologies* is a landmark text for understanding debates about the role of culture in society from the mid-twentieth century onwards.

Who Was Roland Barthes?

The author of *Mythologies*, Roland Gérard Barthes (1915–80), was a French writer, semiotician* (someone who studies the theory of signs* and symbols), and cultural and literary critic, best known for his analyses of French culture, his writings on authorship, and his contributions to photography theory. Barthes was an outsider in society as well as in academic circles: he was secretly gay and worked for a long time in the margins of academic institutions. Suffering from chronic bouts of tuberculosis, his professional advancement was slow. He only got his first permanent job at the age of 45, but by the time he died—after being hit by a laundry van on a street in Paris—he was professor at the Collège de France, the highest position in the French academic system. More importantly, Barthes had become a cultural institution, one of the key voices in French thought, and one of the major theorists of culture of the twentieth century.

Barthes's work pioneered ideas about the systems of signification* operating within culture—that is, on how cultural artifacts such as paintings, advertisements, clothing, and so on convey meaning in societies. His ideas have become the foundations on which much modern-day critical theory* (roughly, a fusion of philosophy and social analysis) has been built.

Although he was associated with the philosophical movements of structuralism* (very roughly, a theoretical approach to culture founded on the idea that culture comes from, and is given meaning by, larger "natural" structures understandable as oppositional pairs such as "raw" and "cooked") and poststructuralism* (an approach that severs culture's connection with these hypothetical structures and the idea of objective truth altogether), he did not commit fully to either movement, instead using his voice to offer critique from the margins of the academic establishment.

His work was tremendously diverse, ranging from semiotic theory and autobiography, to theories about the practice of writing and photography. The one constant that ran throughout his work was his interest in exposing systems of signs within culture. His long-term legacy lay in the field of literature, where he influenced a generation of writers in France and beyond. He removed literature from its pedestal as a higher form of culture and established it as simply another signifying practice (roughly, a way of "making meaning") among many.

What Does *Mythologies* Say?

Mythologies is a collection of short essays on a wide range of subjects drawn from everyday French life: advertisements, national pastimes, marketing of soap powders and detergents, the world of wrestling and many others. Barthes argues that it is possible to read these common objects and experiences as being full of meaning—what he calls the myths of daily life. In this context, Barthes understood myths to be a series of collective beliefs that seem natural and universal, but are, in fact, socially and historically determined.

For Barthes, myths are the delusions of daily life: they are messages, practices, and beliefs that, by social convention, we accept as normal parts of our lives without seeing that they really represent the interests of powerful social groups, in particular the petite bourgeoisie.* The petite bourgeoisie, or little bourgeoisie, should be distinguished from the bourgeoisie,* or big bourgeoisie. Whilst the bourgeoisie, in its Marxist* sense, refers to the owners of the means of production (the tools and resources that laborers need for their work), for Barthes the petite bourgeoisie is made up of the French lower middle classes that work for the bourgeoisie, such as the professionals whose consumer habits help make the business owners rich.

Barthes suggests that in bourgeois society ordinary images and objects like French wine or the Eiffel Tower are, first, taken over and then treated as timeless and universal as a way to protect their place in society. He shows how images and objects are taken out of their history—that is, all context and important information is removed, leaving just the image (or sign), which can then be repackaged as part of specific ideology (that is, roughly, a system of beliefs). These emptied messages are what Barthes calls "myths," and he argues that the process of creating a mythology around collections of these images drains the truth and history out of social interactions, and denies cultural objects and ideas their historical specificity.

In *Mythologies*, Barthes sets out to show how the dominant petit-bourgeois ideology in France presented itself through mass culture as a natural, unquestionable way of ordering of the world. Barthes sees myth as taking over the ordinary objects and acts of everyday French life to spread a petit-bourgeois ideology. What does this mean? That the most basic images can be invested with a second layer of meaning that comes through social usage. Images are then repackaged and placed in a new and totally different context. French wine, for example, becomes more than a drink in its mythological form: it is filled with specific cultural meanings, such as being a representation of the sophisticated values of French society, and the consumption of wine becomes a way of participating in this collective belief. There is nothing naturally sophisticated about wine, but the myth of wine drinking would make it seem as if the beverage's sophistication and glamour were facts of nature.

To summarize, Barthes's central argument is that in French society basic cultural objects such as wine are transformed into universal signs representing specific values of the petite bourgeoisie. He proposes that the myths spread by bourgeois culture homogenize human interactions so that they become timeless and universal ideas that deny their historical context and actual cultural content. In his words, "myth is constituted by the loss of the historical quality of things: in it, things lose the memory that they were once made."[1]

Why Does *Mythologies* Matter?

At its heart, *Mythologies* is a criticism of the petite bourgeoisie; it aims to expose the hidden meanings that support the privileged position that the petite bourgeoisie holds in society. The uniqueness of Barthes's approach is that he expresses his argument by approaching social analysis through semiotics—the study of signs and symbols and their use in communication. Building on work by the father of modern semiotics, the Swiss linguist* Ferdinand de Saussure,* Barthes defined myths as "second-order significations."

If signification is, roughly, the process through which things such as paintings, advertisements, and clothes come to mean something, "second-order signification" is, to put it simply, the making of *new* meanings from things that *already mean something* ("units of meaning"). Using an approach drawn from the field of linguistics (the study of language as a subject in itself), Barthes analyzed the ideological messages transmitted and reinforced by the media and popular culture.

For the full social and political implications of the text to come into view, *Mythologies* should be read through a framework in which readers combine the theoretical study of *semiotics*—the workings of signs and symbols—with a *sociological* view of their function. This approach will allow readers to connect the study of myths to the study of social and cultural history, and to connect the ways in which the creation of a system of myths—the creation of a mythology, that is— works towards satisfying the interests of a capitalist economy.

Mythologies retains its usefulness as a reference point in discussions of culture. It was pioneering in the way it treated the objects of mass culture to genuine critical analysis. Barthes's broad mix of interests and inspirations reflected a new approach to culture that paved the way for the present-day discipline of cultural studies. An abridged English translation of *Mythologies* has been available since 1972, but this left out 25 of Barthes's original essays. As if to confirm its long-lasting importance, the complete *Mythologies* essays were translated into English for the first time in 2013.

Although the individual essays in *Mythologies* are highly entertaining in themselves, offering insightful commentaries on modern life, students should read *Mythologies* for its concluding theoretical essay "Myth Today." This essay gives the collection a coherent overall argument through its development of an analytical method, which, in turn, stresses the importance of Barthes's commentary on French popular culture. His aim is to prevent people from uncritically accepting the messages fed to them by consumer culture. The importance of this activity extends beyond academic study, posing the question of what would happen if we nurtured wiser and more critically engaged citizens in the world.

NOTES

1   Roland Barthes, *Mythologies*, trans. Annette Lavers (London: Vintage, 2000), 142.

SECTION 1
INFLUENCES

MODULE 1
THE AUTHOR AND THE HISTORICAL CONTEXT

KEY POINTS

- *Mythologies* was a groundbreaking work of literary and cultural criticism that had a big impact when it was published in France in 1957.
- Barthes was deeply shaped by his long periods of illness, which affected his career and led to long periods of poverty.
- Barthes's poverty and homosexuality both shaped the ways he responded to consumer culture.

Why Read This Text?

In *Mythologies* (1957), Roland Barthes sketches out a pioneering model through which to analyze the varied signs* of modern culture through the lens of semiotics*—the study of symbols and signs. In semiotics, a sign is, very simply, something that conveys *meaning*. It is the fusion of a "signifier,"* which might be a printed word or an image, and a "signified,"* which is the idea it is communicating.

The collection was revolutionary; it made a great impact on its publication—and ended a long period of instability in Barthes's career, too, establishing his reputation as a promising figure in French intellectual life. Barthes would subsequently reach the summit of this world, and *Mythologies* can be seen as the work that started his rise. Since the 1960s it has also been one of Barthes's most successful and widely read texts, becoming a key companion for generations of students of literature and culture. Almost 60 years have passed since its publication but it remains young and relevant, and a reference point in discussing consumer culture.

> **"** Facts of biography have often provided the psycho-critic with material for explaining underlying (unconscious) aspects of a writer's *oeuvre*. Barthes, however, takes them in hand and uses them as the raw material of his own writing, and even of his style. **"**
>
> John Lechte, *Fifty Key Contemporary Thinkers*

Although Barthes quickly moved on from the ideas set out in *Mythologies*, the book is key to understanding his wider literary and theoretical aims, as well as the movements in literary and cultural criticism appearing in France in the mid-1950s. In it we see all sides of Barthes: the critic, the satirist, the writer, as well as the debunker of the myths of his day.

Author's Life

Roland Gérard Barthes was born in the French naval town of Cherbourg in 1915, to a sailor father and a stay-at-home mother. His mother, Henriette Barthes, was widowed within a year of Roland's birth, when her husband died in naval combat in the North Sea during World War I.* At this point, they moved to the city of Bayonne to live with her husband's family. His maternal grandfather, Louis Gustave Binger, had been an officer who served in France's overseas colonies and who published some highly influential accounts of explorations in West Africa.

Barthes's biographer Louis-Jean Calvet has noted that his childhood in Bayonne was full of boredom and loneliness.[1] Calvet notes the importance during these years of music—Barthes's aunt was a piano teacher—as well as the impact of the bourgeois* (roughly, comfortable middle-class) attitudes of provincial life that he saw around him. Eventually, Barthes and his mother moved to Paris, where his mother became a bookbinder and Roland enrolled in the lyceé—

the secondary school that prepares French students for university.

He was a good student and when he got his baccalauréat,* the high school leaving certificate, he hoped to enroll at the École Normale Supérieure, one of France's elite universities. Tuberculosis, however, forced him to set university aside in order to seek treatment in the Pyrenees mountains of southwest France. A year later he returned to Paris to start his studies in French, Latin, and Greek, but the tuberculosis returned and he spent the following five years in a clinic in the Alps, where he read a great deal, becoming a follower of the French philosopher Jean-Paul Sartre* and a Marxist.* When he finally recovered, he had a string of language-teaching posts abroad, first in Romania and later in Egypt, where he was introduced to the work of the Swiss scholar Ferdinand de Saussure,* a pioneer of modern linguistics*—the study of language.

Barthes left Egypt in 1950 and returned to France, where he began a new job in the Cultural Affairs section of the foreign ministry. He obtained a scholarship to write a thesis in lexicology,* the study of the origin and meaning of words, but made little progress with his research. Instead, he published his first work of literary criticism, *Writing Degree Zero* (1953), and began writing regular articles on French culture of the day for literary magazines, including *Les Lettres nouvelles*. The brief essays written for this publication would later be collected as *Mythologies*.

Author's Background

The most important influences on Barthes's life were a lack of money, illness, professional uncertainty, and his sexuality. Although he came from a middle-class family, his father's death brought the family serious financial hardship. Barthes experienced long periods of poverty during his upbringing, which caused him great embarrassment. This situation did not improve when he became an adult, as his frequent tuberculosis prevented him from going into an academic career on two occasions. In many ways, his illness decided what kind of life he would be able to lead: one of limited physical movement and financial resources, but rich in thought—a kind of cultured poverty. Unable to have an academic career, Barthes experienced long periods of uncertainty about his career: between the mid-1940s and mid-1960s he lived off short-term writing and teaching jobs, with no clear sense of direction or the hope of a steady job. He was suspicious of academic institutions and even when he worked within them years later, he never fully took advantage of his rising fame.

Barthes was gay, and tried to keep his sexuality a secret during his lifetime. In his memoir, he described how his principal "formative problem was doubtless money, not sex."[2] Indeed, his long experience of financial strain explains his response to consumer culture in *Mythologies*: he was fascinated with the attraction of commercial culture, even though he remained critical of it. Barthes may have downplayed the importance of his own sexuality, but expressing it was central to *Mythologies*. In the essays, Barthes wrote suggestively about the sensuous side of consumer culture, such as in his commentary on the displays of male virility in the bodies of wrestlers. Perhaps most tellingly, his essay on striptease points, in a hidden way, to his own inability to make public his sexuality by warning of the dangers of insincere expressions of sexuality.

NOTES

1   Louis-Jean Calvet, *Roland Barthes: A Biography*, trans. Sarah Wykes (Cambridge: Polity Press, 1994), 15.

2   Roland Barthes, *Roland Barthes by Roland Barthes*, trans. Richard Howard (New York: Hill & Wang, 1977), 45.

MODULE 2
ACADEMIC CONTEXT

KEY POINTS

- With *Mythologies*, Barthes wrote about culture in a tense and uncertain period in France, which saw rapid modernization, a bitter colonial war, and the rise of the bourgeois* class (roughly, the middle class).

- Barthes and his fellow leftist intellectual the philosopher Jean-Paul Sartre* both found themselves politically frustrated—critical of France's growing bourgeois society but repelled by the brutal communism* of the Soviet* bloc.

- Barthes had an uneasy relationship with France's mostly conservative academic institutions. During the 1950s most of Barthes's intellectual activity was as a journalist.

The Work in its Context

Roland Barthes's *Mythologies* came from a series of monthly columns he wrote between 1954 and 1956 for the literary magazine *Les Lettres nouvelles*. These columns were then collected and published as a single volume, which included an additional theoretical essay, "Myth Today." Later, more of the columns were published in two English-language collections, *Mythologies* and *The Eiffel Tower* (1964). It is important to remember this publication history when considering the work's context.

In *Mythologies* Barthes looked to remove the divide between popular (journalism) and elite (academic) forms of writing. He wrote about French society for a wide readership. He talked about linguistics* (the study of language and its structure) and the new disciplines of structuralism* (a theoretical approach that assumes that we arrive at

> 66 In phrases that echo Marx of *The Eighteenth Brumaire of Louis Bonaparte*, Barthes characterizes bourgeois ideology as an exercise in ex-nomination in which bourgeois reality is dissolved in a vocabulary that is universalistic. 99
>
> Eugene Goodheart, *The Skeptic Disposition in Contemporary Criticism*

meaning in a culture by drawing on larger "natural" oppositional pairs such as "day and night") and semiology* (the study of signs* and symbols). But his main concerns were social and political. Indeed, although Barthes looked to the ways in which these disciplines approached the study of language and communication, he used their methods to develop a new form of popular social criticism through the study of images of French society.

Barthes entered the scene during the 1950s, an uncertain period in France. On one level, the French statesman Charles de Gaulle* was attempting to restore a sense of national pride in the aftermath of the Nazi* occupation during World War II.* On another, France was suffering from an imperial crisis, engaged in a bloody war with its north African colony of Algeria,* which was fighting for independence. Along with these tense circumstances came a period of rapid modernization, which saw the spread of mass culture and rising living standards of the French middle classes. This prosperity led to the social, political, and cultural dominance of a new class: the petite bourgeoisie* or little bourgeoisie.

Barthes took and expanded the term bourgeoisie from classical Marxism* (the social analysis of the German economist and political theorist Karl Marx).* In its Marxist sense, it referred to business owners, or capitalists,* as distinct from the proletariat,* the wage earners whose labor the bourgeoisie exploit. In Barthes's version the petite bourgeoisie also included the lower middle classes, or the world of professionals whose consumerism (their need to purchase more goods and services to fuel their rising living standards) helped the business owners grow rich.

Barthes resented the dominance of the petite bourgeoisie and its values of commercialism and consumerism. In *Mythologies* he attacked bourgeois society from a position of social criticism. He attacked, in particular, the ideological* structures that were at the heart of petite-bourgeois culture, and, in turn, its social and political power. In this way, *Mythologies* captured a whole decade in French life, recording the social effects of changing patterns of cultural consumption of a society becoming fascinated with popular culture.

Overview of the Field

The other figure in French intellectual life who was publically hostile to the consolidation of bourgeois society and culture was the philosopher Jean-Paul Sartre.*

Sartre dominated French intellectual thought in the 1950s, and was the leading figure of the philosophical and literary movement known as Existentialism* (which, very roughly, focuses on the nature and possibilities of human existence). Sartre and Barthes shared a particular political frustration that resulted from the tense Cold War* climate of the time, which made it difficult for left-leaning intellectuals like them to find a political home. Barthes and Sartre were both sharp critics of capitalism in France. But they were also wary of supporting Soviet-influenced communism, especially following the events of 1956, when Russia invaded Hungary to put down a popular revolution against Soviet-imposed communist policies.* Both felt resentful of the seeming lack of political options, and of their inability to support the rigid ideologies of either capitalism or Stalinism,* the particularly repressive style of communism practiced by the Soviet leader Joseph Stalin* until his death in 1953.

In his work *What is Literature?* (1947), Sartre reviewed the position of bourgeois writers in postwar France, and questioned the ethical substance of their writing. The text deals with the notions of commitment and of audience: in other words, for whom does one write?

Sartre believed that writers always wrote for their contemporaries, that is, for fellow members of their class or race. He observed how following the French Revolution* bourgeois writers had reversed their role as communicators of social justice. Instead, they represented the class that was gradually gaining power and, as a result, had the means to enforce social and cultural oppression. Sartre argued that, as a result, modern writers had become alienated, or distanced from their true aims, since their immediate audience had become increasingly dominant and was, therefore, no longer the ideal audience for writings on justice. He suggested that modern bourgeois writers should overcome the barrier of writing for their own class, and instead ground their writing in the writer's commitment to address his or her own freedom as well as the freedom of others.

Barthes responded to *What is Literature?* directly in *Writing Degree Zero* (1953), arguing that the act of writing always presents a choice of values. In addition, *Mythologies* also touches on the question of commitment, but deals with this at a semiological* level—at the level of language—rather than at the level of content or audience.

Academic Influences

Roland Barthes only got his first permanent job in 1960, at the École Pratique des Hautes Études, one of France's most elite universities. He was forty-five, and this job ended decades of financial and professional uncertainty. During the 1950s Barthes was, above all, a journalist, and most of his intellectual activity was writing for particular journals. Along with his column for *Les Lettres nouvelles* he also co-founded a radical journal dedicated to theater called *Théâtre populaire*. These two journals reflected their era, notably in their criticisms of the Algerian

War, in which France tried brutally, but unsuccessfully, to keep control of its colony. The two journals also showed Barthes's basic vision, in which he aimed to unite his political critique with the development of new approaches to literary and linguistic theory.

Barthes had an uneasy relationship with the stifling orthodoxy of academic institutions in France, such as the Sorbonne, a university known for its traditional, and in some ways conservative, approach to education and scholarship. Barthes felt the best way to construct a left-leaning theoretical framework to analyze French society was by writing journalism, since it existed beyond academic control.

MODULE 3
THE PROBLEM

KEY POINTS

- *Mythologies* is a book about French identity and how it was being shaped by the myths spread by popular culture.

- Barthes agreed with such writers as the German cultural critics Theodor Adorno* and Max Horkheimer* that mass culture quietly promotes narrow-minded commercial values. But unlike those writers, he was also fascinated with mass culture.

- *Mythologies* was influenced by the Swiss linguistics* scholar Ferdinand de Saussure* and the French anthropologist Claude Lévi-Strauss,* and was a sort of bridge between the former's semiology* (the study of signs* and symbols) and the latter's social analysis.

Core Question

Many of the themes Roland Barthes addresses in *Mythologies* are particular to France. At its core, *Mythologies* is a book about French identity: it is a personal reaction to the lies that Barthes felt French society was telling about itself. As such, it had a political agenda, tracing Barthes's frustrations with the social and political landscape in France, and, in particular, the French public's willingness to buy into the myths spread by popular culture, politicians, and the media. While most of the myths supported small-minded petit-bourgeois* values, others promoted more worrying trends, such as the anti-intellectualism[1] and racism spread by the powerful extreme-right politician Pierre Poujade.*

The core of *Mythologies* is the questioning of how meaning is

> 66 One of the most notable cultural shifts during the advent of advanced capitalism is this move from a market organized around individual categories of products to one organized around buyers investing in diverse and multifaceted 'images,' and for whom the actual consumer goods are nothing but a single element in a more general economy of self-identification. 99
>
> Peter Gibian, "On/Against Mass Culture Theories"

distorted in everyday politics and mass culture. Barthes places in context a simple form of ideological* manipulation. He examines how manufactured culture and particular values are presented as if they are natural, unquestioned, and universal. Barthes is motivated less by a chance to condemn the spreading of such myths than by trying to understand the willingness of people to blindly accept the spectacles offered to them.

The Participants

The widespread influence of mass popular culture was a postwar development in France. It was also felt in other European countries and in North America. As a result, the very idea of culture was changing, caught in a midway space between the high art of modernism* (a movement in the arts from the late nineteenth to the mid-twentieth century that broke with traditional notions of art) and the emerging practices of postmodernism* (a later style and conceptual approach to art and culture that emerged in the second half of the twentieth century). This fueled interest in the study of culture as a driving force in society, a shift in approach to the historical study of culture that is commonly referred to as the cultural turn.*

As the American cultural historian Michael Denning explains, "with the discovery that culture was everywhere, the study and critique of culture became an increasingly central part of political and intellectual life."[2] Over a period of 30 years, several key works looked for meaning in the new languages of mass culture, such as the German cultural critic Walter Benjamin's* "The Work of Art in the Age of Mechanical Reproduction" (1935), Raymond Williams's* *Culture and Society* (1958), and Marshall McLuhan's* *Understanding Media* (1964).

Mythologies is best positioned alongside another important work: Theodor W. Adorno and Max Horkheimer's "The Culture Industry: Enlightenment as Mass Deception" (1944). This essay is one of the most powerful expressions of contempt for mass culture. In it, Adorno and Horkheimer use a Marxist* framework to propose that through a series of regulatory processes that include the standardization of cultural material—such as radio, film, and magazines—and the carefully managed distribution of this material, culture was turned into a commodity—that is, a product to be sold.

In the culture industry, culture and advertising blend, making it difficult to see where art ends and sales propaganda begins. In this context, the mass media becomes a technology of totalitarian* power—that is, through it, all aspects of the citizen's life are made subject to governmental authority. It does this by absorbing expressions of individuality into the dominant social, political, and economic system, which is highly regulated. In Horkheimer and Adorno's view, the culture industry is essentially a repressive system that creates a false sense of individuality and hides the repression it supports behind the language of freedom.

Like Adorno and Horkheimer, Barthes analyzes popular culture using familiar Marxist themes: ideology* (a system of beliefs held with a political intent), class, commodity fetishism* (roughly, the belief that a product's value is in the status it confers rather than in its utility), and authenticity. *Mythologies* questions what kind of ideologies emerge from popular culture, and goes on to attack the "bourgeois* norm" as the "essential enemy."[3] Barthes follows Adorno and Horkheimer's lead by declaring the act of critique the basis of a progressive social and political act. He calls for rereading and reinterpreting familiar cultural images to expose them as not merely pretty, clever, or entertaining artistic creations, but as carriers of a particular ideology. However, in contrast to Adorno and Horkheimer, Barthes makes a serious critique of both high culture and mass culture. In *Mythologies* Barthes shows both revulsion for parts of popular culture and a genuine fascination with it. As such, the book signals an important turning point in cultural criticism, for it promotes the study of new cultural phenomena from a position of partial acceptance, rather than straightforward opposition.

The Contemporary Debate

Until *Mythologies*, Barthes was unknown in French intellectual circles. His health had prevented him from taking up a permanent academic job, and he earned a poor living writing for journals for many years. This kept him from carrying out research and leading a full intellectual life. Although he was briefly associated with the philosophy of existentialism* and the theoretical school of structuralism,* he watched their development from the sidelines without becoming fully involved with either movement. In some ways Barthes can be seen as a bridge between the thinkers of these two generations, rather than a central participant.

Barthes initially admired the existentialist philosopher Jean-Paul Sartre.* But he ended up distancing himself from him in the mid-1950s following Sartre's partial support for Stalinism.* It was then that Barthes turned to serious academic study and became interested in the work of the linguist Ferdinand de Saussure. Saussure had developed the academic discipline of semiology: the study of signs and symbols.

Saussure's theories were very influential for structuralists such as the anthropologist Claude Lévi-Strauss, who argued in "The Structural Study of Myth,"[4] that myth functions as a language. In the concluding section of *Mythologies*, entitled "Myth Today," Barthes built on Saussure's ideas to argue that everyday activities such as drinking wine or driving a particular car could also be thought of as carrying ideological and other messages. In this sense, Barthes combined Saussure and Lévi-Strauss's structuralist ideas, bringing together semiology with social analysis to study a French society that was changing itself as it became more and more a modern consumer society.

NOTES

1   See the essay "Poujade and the Intellectuals," in Roland Barthes, *The Eiffel Tower and Other Mythologies*, trans. Richard Howard (London: University of California Press, 1997), 127–36.

2   Michael Denning, *Culture in the Age of Three Worlds* (London: Verso, 2004), 2.

3   Roland Barthes, "Preface to the 1970 Edition," in *Mythologies*, trans. Annette Lavers (London: Vintage, 2000), 9.

4   See Claude Lévi-Strauss, "The Structural Study of Myth," *The Journal of American Folklore* 68, no. 270 (1955): 428–44.

MODULE 4
THE AUTHOR'S CONTRIBUTION

KEY POINTS

- In *Mythologies,* Roland Barthes argued that popular culture was replacing religion and cultural traditions in shaping values and ideas in postwar France. He set about trying to analyze how this took place.

- Barthes combined linguistic* theory with Marxist* social criticism to analyze the messages of common cultural phenomena—films, photographs, advertisements—in a new light.

- In the same way that Sigmund Freud* showed that the surface stories of dreams hide deeper messages, Barthes argued that popular culture of postwar France often carried hidden messages in support of nationalism, racism, and a social order based on social classes.

Author's Aims

In *Mythologies* Roland Barthes sees the explosion of mass culture in French society as a new form of psychological influence, shaping citizens' lives in a deep way. He proposes that the values of postwar France were not being determined by religion or cultural traditions. Instead, values were shaped by the trivia of popular culture, such as the haircuts of film stars and advertisements for detergents.

Barthes calls these fragments of culture "myths." In a series of short essays, *Mythologies* sets out to determine the rules of their functioning and reveal the limits of their influence. In short, Barthes's project was to decode the structure of myth by defining it.

Barthes was not the only writer working on decoding culture in

> **❝**The structuralist idea that meaning is agreed rather than determinate challenged the idea that … the architecture of a cathedral is in some way more meaningful than the design of a car. … Rather, it is simply that a powerful group of people—the French bourgeoisie—agreed at the time that the cathedral had more artistic value. In … *Mythologies,* [Barthes] was able to argue that, like the great Gothic cathedrals, cars had become 'the supreme creation of an era.' In other words the Gothic cathedrals and Citroën cars have meaning only within the myth structures of their own time. **❞**
>
> Christopher Routledge, *Key Thinkers in Linguistics and the Philosophy of Language*

the 1950s. His friend Henri Lefebvre* had also critiqued the rise of mass culture in *Critique of Everyday Life* (1947). Lefebvre suggested that the experience of everyday life could be the focus of critical analysis. He considered the role ordinary experiences played in life in postwar France, and considered the way the structure of the everyday was being shaped by capitalism.* Both writers treated popular culture theoretically, looking to expose its underlying structures. However, the similarities between the two were superficial, as Barthes's approach to cultural analysis was different.[1] Whereas Lefebvre focused on environments, *Mythologies* was unique in the way that it presented a social argument through semiotics.* He felt that this type of analysis would allow familiar objects and everyday experiences to be understood with a new clarity.

Approach

Barthes's approach changed the way in which the language of culture was talked about by defining myth as "*a form of speech* … a system of communication."[2] It is important to clarify that Barthes did not propose that all language was myth, or, conversely, that myth was limited to language. He expanded the definition of myth so that almost any form of communication could become myth: words, images, films, photographs, advertisements. In addition, by turning to linguistics through which to analyze French culture, he showed that the process of analysis itself could be a politically progressive act.

The connections Barthes sketches between language and social theory contributed to the development of a form of structuralist* analysis. Structuralism was an approach to the study of culture that considered all elements of knowledge to make up a system of interrelated parts, or signs.* Structuralists maintained that all human activity has meaning because it operates within a system made up of related parts. Barthes's argument is structuralist in the way that it focuses on form rather than content, in particular the manner through which cultural objects and experiences promote certain meanings by concealing others.

Barthes's structuralist analysis, then, had a semiological* foundation (with its emphasis on signs), and a Marxist* political agenda (with its critique of capitalist society).

Contribution in Context

Barthes borrowed heavily from Ferdinand de Saussure's* model of linguistics. To describe the way myths are communicated, he adopted several of Saussure's terms: the signifier* (the form in which an idea is transmitted, such as a printed word or image), the signified* (the idea being communicated by a signifier), and the sign (the combination of the material signifier and the signified). These elements all contribute to the process of signification,* which in Saussure's terms, refers to the process of conveying meaning through linguistic signs. Barthes used Saussure's terms, but he proposed that myths work at a second order of signification.

What does this mean? Well, for Saussure, the semiological chain of *signifier* + *signified* = *sign* was a process of signification (of making meaning) that was complete. So, in Saussure's model, the combination of the signifier *roses* (the word or mental image of a bouquet of roses) with the signified roses (the cultural concept of roses meaning "romance") produces a complete sign: roses are a sign of romance and can be printed on Valentine's cards to signify this meaning. And that is where it ends.

But for Barthes, that is where a myth begins. A myth is a complete sign (the combination of a signifier such as the word "roses" and a signified such as the cultural concept of roses meaning "romance") that becomes a new signifier for a new signified: that is, *a new concept or associative meaning*. This is what is meant by a "second order of signification."

In mythology, Saussure's sign is not the culmination of a process of meaning; rather, it is the starting point for questioning the underlying logic of the signifying system of which the sign is part. Barthes suggests that there is no intrinsic reason why roses should signify romance, and proposes that the meaning of the sign is empty until we understand the process that led to its creation. The second, mythological order reveals the process by which roses have come to signify romance. Whereas for Saussure signification is the final product of linguistic analysis, for Barthes signification is the myth itself.

To avoid confusion, Barthes adapted Saussure's terminology: the signifier became "form," the signified "concept," and the sign "signification."[3] In order to explain these terms in relation to myth, Barthes compared Saussure's system of language to the system of dreams proposed by the founder of psychoanalysis, Sigmund Freud. Like Freud's dreams, which are made up of impressions drawn from daily activities, myths are made up of the coded messages used by a particular society. These elements—which he termed "raw material(s)"[4]—represent the form/signifier of each system. The mental associations that dreams call forth, or, in the case of myth, the cultural meanings they evoke, are, in each case, the concept/signified. The combination of these two elements, that is, the "manifest" or surface content, and the "latent or hidden content," produces the final meaning: the sign or signification of either dream or myth.

For Barthes, what sets myths apart from dreams is their ideological* content; myths are types of speech that are ideologically charged. It is at this point that Barthes develops the structural transformations from first order to second order of signification, and from there he develops his social theory. Like repressed thoughts in dreams, the signs of culture carry unconscious or hidden meanings that signify something else beyond their surface meaning or first order of signification—that is, beyond what culture makes to seem natural.

Barthes understood "myth" to have two meanings. The first is a collective legend used to explain natural or social phenomena. The second is a lie, or a widely held but false belief or idea: myth is a form of mystification.

NOTES

1   For an article considering the similarities and differences between the two writers, see Michael Kelly, "Demystification: A Dialogue between Barthes and Lefebvre," *Yale French Studies* 98 (2000): 79–97.

2   Roland Barthes, *Mythologies*, trans. Annette Lavers (London: Vintage, 2000), 109.

3   Barthes, *Mythologies*, 117.

4   Barthes, *Mythologies*, 114.

SECTION 2
IDEAS

MAIN IDEAS

KEY POINTS

- In *Mythologies*, Barthes looks critically at everyday life in postwar France and reveals how common objects and experiences carry particular messages and values that consumers are generally unaware of receiving.

- The central idea of *Mythologies* is that the messages transmitted by culture are never innocent; they are always charged with ideological* values or meanings (that is, they represent some sort of political ideology).

- *Mythologies* presents its ideas in a series of short analytical essays and one final theoretical one, which gives the whole collection an overall message and points to the social importance of decoding myths.

Key Themes

In *Mythologies*, Roland Barthes examines the messages transmitted by the mass media in post-World War II* France. Barthes calls these messages myths, and he analyzes them linguistically,* breaking down their operation as a semiotic* system: that is, his analysis draws on theory related to the structure of language that explains how meaning is transmitted through linguistic signs.*

For his part, Barthes addresses a wide selection of familiar objects and experiences drawn from everyday French life—the world of professional wrestling, the famous bicycle race known as the Tour de France,* steak and fries, film-star Greta Garbo's* face—and treats them all as cultural objects that can be analyzed critically. His central argument is that the functioning of popular culture builds up a

> **❝** For ... Barthes ... myth (or ideology) is what transforms history into Nature by lending arbitrary signs as apparently obvious, unalterable set of connotations ... The 'naturalization' thesis is here extended to discourse as such, rather than to the world of which it speaks. The 'healthy' sign for Barthes is one which unashamedly displays its own gratuitousness, the fact that there is no internal or self-evident bond between itself and what it represents; and to this extent artistic modernism, which typically broods upon the 'unmotivated' nature of its own sign-systems, emerges as politically progressive. **❞**
>
> Terry Eagleton, *Ideology: An Introduction*

mythology: a collection of widely held beliefs that help explain the values of a given society.

Barthes proposes that these myths, which are routinely accepted as natural and ahistorical—that is, they are not determined by any specific historical context—in fact communicate particular social and political messages. The key themes that *Mythologies* examines are: the consumption of mass media and popular culture; the demystification of the everyday; the linguistic study of signs or myths; and the opposition between the essential nature of things and the ideological meanings they have taken on.

Barthes's analysis of myth also looks at the key role of the cultural critic. He argues that the general public consumes myths innocently, receiving the messages fed to it through the cultural outlets of capitalist* economies (newspapers, TV, Hollywood films) as though they were universal images of the world. By this he means that consumers of myths—such as readers of tabloid newspapers—are not aware that myths are socially, historically, and politically determined, and accept them as natural parts of life. In contrast, the semiotic analysis of myths undertaken by the cultural critic exposes the fact that the myths are constructed by particular groups in a particular historical and economic context.

For Barthes, this act of critical analysis is equivalent to a political gesture. By exposing the myths of any given society, the cultural critic becomes a kind of revolutionary who contributes to the liberation of language from the many myths that make up a national culture.

Exploring the Ideas

Mythologies has a central theme: signs within culture are never innocent; rather, they are part of complex systems of ideological signification*— they transmit a particular ideology or values.

Barthes examines this theme by exploring a series of mythologies in French life through a semiological lens, that is, analyzing the signs through which its meaning is carried, in each case showing that what appears to be natural and neutral is not so. He develops a theory of signs to account for this deception, suggesting that the construction of myths produces two levels of signification: a first-order linguistic system, which he calls the "*language-object*," and a second-order system that transmits the myth, which he terms a "*metalanguage.*"[1]

The first-order language-object is "the language which myth gets hold of in order to build its own system";[2] in other words, it is the literal or explicit meaning of things, or what is known in linguistics as the realm of denotation.* The second order is made up of the language that is used to *speak* about the denotative language of the first order. As such, this second-order language is a metalanguage—because it speaks about another language—and it exists in the realm of connotation* (that is, as a type of language that is used to refer to the social, cultural, and ideological associations or meanings of signs).

The distinction between denotation and connotation is a key theme in *Mythologies*. While the first order of denotation refers to the literal or supposedly self-evident meaning of things, the second order of connotation and myth describes the added layers of mythological meanings that become attached to them, or the implied meanings. So, for example, an advertisement for a car will operate with two layers of meaning. The ad might show a man driving a convertible car fast down a countryside road with a younger woman in the passenger seat. At the first-order level, the relationship between all the ad's elements (man, woman, car, countryside) is assumed to be objective and value free. However, there is a second layer of meaning—the level of connotations, or myth, where the signs take on the value system of the culture in which they are used. At this level, the ad may express such values as individualism, escape from the stresses of the city, power, or sexual prowess.

Barthes argues that connotations are not static and can vary between cultures. There is nothing essentially positive about the countryside or negative about the city, but the myth the ad proposes would make it seem that this understanding is a fact of nature. With this, Barthes emphasizes that meaning is always culturally determined. He proposes that the level of connotation is cynical, for it seeks to make ideological propositions appear as the natural way things are.

Barthes draws attention to the ways in which mythological connotations make themselves seem self-evident. He proposes that readers do not notice the complicated systems of signification at work and argues that consumers of myth take messages at face value, reading only the first-order meanings: "the myth-consumer takes the signification for a system of facts: myth is read as a factual system, whereas it is but a semiological system."[3]

Language and Expression

Mythologies can be broken down broadly into two parts. The first is a collection of short essays on features of French culture in the 1950s in which Barthes decodes their real significance as bearers of social meanings. The second is an extended essay called "Myth Today," in which Barthes defines myth and describes a semiotic model with which to explain how cultural texts (images, for example, or pop songs) can transmit several levels of meaning.

As a result of its structure, the first part of *Mythologies* reads like a collection of small insights, rather than a coherent whole. But the long concluding essay "Myth Today" brings the whole together and gives the text direction by developing Barthes's analytical method in greater depth. It also shows the critical importance of this type of analysis: to prevent people from accepting the cultural messages they are fed as natural.

Barthes's semiotic approach to social analysis makes the style of *Mythologies* highly distinctive as a reading of popular culture with terms taken from the technical vocabularies of linguistics, sociology, and philosophy. The tone of the essays is one of both fascination and revulsion (sometimes in uneasy coexistence) for the objects of popular culture.

NOTES

1   Roland Barthes, *Mythologies*, trans. Annette Lavers (London: Vintage, 2000), 115.

2   Barthes, *Mythologies*, 115.

3   Barthes, *Mythologies*, 131.

MODULE 6
SECONDARY IDEAS

KEY POINTS

- The principal secondary idea in *Mythologies* is that myths remove history from culture and language. Images become empty so they can be repackaged with the values of the socially dominant group in society.

- Barthes emphasizes the ideological* context in myths, showing how meaning always reflects the interests of a particular social grouping.

- Barthes's study of myth can also be read as a chronicle of postwar France.

Other Ideas

One of the key secondary ideas put forward by Roland Barthes in *Mythologies* is that myths remove history from language. This is a complex idea, which refers to how the way we speak about cultural images and objects takes out their historical content. This historical content is what Barthes understands to be an image's specific contextual information—such as where or when the image was produced and for what purpose. The removal of history is achieved by hiding the process of signification* in communication—that is, by hiding the process by which meaning is conveyed; signification here means the process of connecting a signifier* (or "form," in Barthes's terminology) to a signified* (or "concept").

By removing this connection, Barthes proposes that myths remove all the context and specific information from signs,* turning them into "an empty, parasitical form."[1] In other words, signs can be turned into empty images that can be repackaged to transmit different sets of

> ❝ Mythic signification has political dimensions. It is precisely the function of myth to depoliticize the uses of meaning by 'naturalizing' them—that is, turning them into eternal essences beyond question. Naturalization disguises the fact that myth is chosen ... from among a variety of options ... Myth, then, is a tool by which the bourgeoisie keeps at bay the Revolution. The bourgeoisie wish to maintain a status quo in which their power is secured. ❞
>
> Milton Scarborough, *Myth and Modernity: Postcritical Reflections*

meanings from those they had originally, denying them their historical uniqueness. Barthes thinks of this process as a kind of "*arrest*," a process that slows down the process of signification, freezing particular meanings into an "eternal reference" that serves "to *establish*" social meanings. These meanings are homogenized—that is, standardized, and made out to be universal.[2]

Exploring the Ideas

In one of the most famous essays in *Mythologies*, Barthes describes an image of a black soldier saluting a French flag. The concept of this image is French military strength, and by showing "blackness" and "Frenchness" together, on the surface it serves to signify the impartiality, or lack of prejudice, of French culture.

But Barthes suggests that beyond this first level of signification the image has removed the signifier of the black soldier from its real history—the long, troubled, and violent history of French colonial exploitation—and inserted it into an entirely different system of myth. Barthes proposes that this mythological system denies the actual history of exploitation in favor of an alternative meaning: the concept of a fair and unprejudiced vision of French culture and France's empire. In this way, through a process of deforming history and meaning, the soldier now becomes the sign of French impartiality or fair play. The image has been emptied of the true imperial history that it should connote—an imperial history of violence and exploitation—and is reduced to an empty image.

What this example shows is that even though myths have many potential signifiers, they are treated as essential views of the world that mean something in and of themselves. To paraphrase Barthes, myth takes out the fullness of the concept it is speaking about in order to homogenize it. Barthes, however, observes how this emptying is also a kind of filling, for even as myth attempts to turn the concept into a timeless, essential meaning, it always gives the sign an entire history, perspective, and prejudice of its own. This is a key secondary idea, as it shifts Barthes's entire critical approach to the ideological construction of all myth.

With this he emphasizes how meaning is never static or innocent, and always reflects the interests of a particular social group. Thus he moves his project from the study of semiology* (how meaning is conveyed through signs) to the study of ideology (a system of beliefs forming a particular political worldview).

Overlooked

One important aspect often overlooked is that before its publication as a collection, most of *Mythologies*'s essays had already been published in the literary magazine *Les Lettres nouvelles*. Between 1954 and 1956 Barthes contributed a regular column called "Mythology of the Month" to the magazine, in which he examined diverse aspects of everyday life. *Mythologies* is most commonly taken as a work of cultural theory, but seeing it this way allows for it to also be read as a chronicle of postwar France.

Barthes's idea of demystifying the cultural messages of society through semiotics and relating those messages to broader social and political questions was radically new. The range of cultural material he drew together was also extraordinary, and allows readers to take away from the text more than Barthes's analytical strategy, shifting focus to the significance of cultural objects themselves.

Some critics have focused on some of the lesser-known themes Barthes addresses. The scholar and translator Kristin Ross has centered on the attention he pays to notions of cleanliness in several of the essays. Ross points to Barthes's analyses of soap powder and laundry detergent to examine how hygiene was elevated to such high status in French domestic life following the Algerian War.* In *Fast Cars, Clean Bodies: Decolonization and the Reordering of French Culture* (1995), Ross uses Barthes to develop a grammar—or way of speaking—of hygiene. Barthes presents hygiene as a language of signs through which it is possible to also think about hygiene as a metaphor for postwar ideas of nationhood in France. Ross develops this understanding to argue that the French obsession with hygiene is a way to transfer the discriminating practices of colonial societies into domestic metropolitan environments. In other words, cleanliness is a means by which the French look to preserve a sense of difference and superiority over the citizens from nations until recently colonized by France.

What does this mean? When Barthes develops grammars for different systems of signs—in other words, when he is analyzing deeper meanings in laundry powder advertisements or magazine covers—he is also analyzing the needs and desires of a particular society coming to terms with modernization. France was undergoing massive change during the 1950s—dealing with the rise of mass culture and mass media, recovering from a world war, losing its last colonial possessions—and *Mythologies* charts how the creation of new consumer desires contribute to the development of a new concept of nation.

Barthes shows how links between everyday life, the ending of France's control over Algeria, and the symbolic power of consumer products connect consumer culture with notions of nationhood. In particular, Barthes analyzes commercial practices to ask what it means to be part of a collective idea of the French nation.

NOTES

1 Roland Barthes, *Mythologies*, trans. Annette Lavers (London: Vintage, 2000), 117.

2 Barthes, *Mythologies*, 125.

MODULE 7
ACHIEVEMENT

KEY POINTS

- *Mythologies* achieved its goal of exposing the myths of the dominant bourgeois* culture. But Barthes worried the work soon lost relevance and did not fully achieve its goal of totally exposing the "sacred" status of signifying* systems (that is, the systems by which meaning is conveyed).

- *Mythologies* breathed new life into Marxist* debates and made it legitimate for academics to study popular culture.

- Barthes's political affiliations prevented him from exposing the Left's own mythological practices with the same critical eye he reserved for the bourgeoisie.

Assessing the Argument

In the preface to the 1970s edition of *Mythologies*, Roland Barthes declared the text's twofold aim. The first was to provide an ideological* critique of the language of mass culture. The second was to analyze the mechanics of this language. Barthes, therefore, intended for the text to move in two directions: one, political, with a clear Marxist orientation, and another, semiological,* drawing on the analytical tools of structuralism* (an approach to the analysis of culture that, roughly, seeks to identify the structural oppositions—"raw/cooked," for example—that serve to allow people to construct meaning). These parallel routes came together with one goal: the development of a political semiology of myth.

Barthes realized his political aim of undermining the culture of the social class known as the petite bourgeoisie by demystifying its sign* systems. He did not, however, develop a full political and economic

66 *Mythologies's* great resonance within the history of mass culture derives ... from ... the very diversity, of commodity practices that Barthes draws on from across a vast range of modern everyday life. To the extent that dominant ideology operates by means of the grafting onto the objects and practices of the world a set of very specific (and circumscribed) values, semiology becomes interlinked with ideology-critique: the mythologist studies bourgeois acts of signification—especially in their internal workings in the construction of socially tendentious meanings—in all sort of things from words and pictures to gadgets and gizmos 99

Dana Polan, "Roland Barthes's *Mythologies:* A Breakthrough Contribution to the Study of Mass Culture"

theory of systems of signs, as he found that his own semiology also had the potential to become myth, and required demystifying as well. For this reason, Barthes felt that in the end, *Mythologies* fell short of realizing its ambitions. Although the dominant bourgeois values and myths, which Barthes described as his "essential enemy,"[1] were undoubtedly undermined by *Mythologies*, their hold over cultural production remained. Yet the need for ideological criticism became ever more urgent with the events of May 1968,* when French workers joined students in a general strike that paralyzed the country and almost brought down the government. Barthes admitted that he had not managed to completely destroy the sign and achieve the *semioclasm** (the undoing of the sacred status of certain signs in the culture of the day) that he wished for in his preface. He realized that his mythology project quickly became historical, overtaken by more nuanced and precise work of semiological analysis, making his own ideas seem static and, themselves, mythological.

Achievement in Context

Mythologies is important for two principal reasons.

First, it created a new avenue for Marxist cultural theory by bringing together the study of semiotics with elements of critical theory* (roughly, a combination of sociology and philosophy). Before the book's publication, neo-Marxists* (people who adapted classical Marxist thought to account for the social changes that occurred since Marx formulated his arguments) were stumbling along in an entirely new, postwar cultural landscape, using concepts inherited from economic and political writings a hundred years old. *Mythologies* brought about an entirely new conceptual vocabulary that gave new life to Marxist discourse.

Second, *Mythologies* made it legitimate for academics to study popular culture. Unlike many of his fellow scholars, Barthes chose not to work with obscure and elevated cultural material, instead illustrating how even the ordinary clutter of popular culture—be it a wrestling match, an advertisement for detergent, or French toys—could be subjected to genuine critical analysis. Barthes gave the objects of popular culture a complexity usually reserved for art or literature. As a result, *Mythologies* destabilized and challenged the boundaries separating high culture from popular culture.

Barthes's contributions to the development of a semiotic form of cultural theory and his giving legitimacy to popular culture proved to be pioneering. *Mythologies* became a key work in cultural studies, and its ideas had a tremendous influence on the discipline in the 1970s, with its analyses of the mechanics of advertising and the media. From that point onward, *Mythologies* became a vital reference point in debates about the field.

Limitations

In *Mythologies* Barthes seeks to expose how myths work by distorting images so that they appear natural, arbitrary, and disconnected from history. Barthes resists notions of universality by proposing that mythologies always carry social and political messages that are determined by a particular history and culture. But Barthes's system of analysis also carries its own limitations. For instance, Barthes limits his discussion of myths to the bourgeoisie* and does not confront the possibility that ideologies on the Left also work by spreading their own complex mythologies.

Mythologies makes it clear that Barthes believes his leftist viewpoint is capable of removing distortion from cultural analysis. Barthes feels that, unlike the bourgeoisie, the Left is capable of analyzing culture in a way that is free from bias, maintaining a fair and objective view of reality. This is an error that Barthes shared with many other Marxist thinkers of the time. In fact, the Left was as deeply engaged in myth-making as the bourgeoisie. In the concluding essay "Myth Today," Barthes dedicates a small section to "Myth on the Left."[2] Here, he accepts that myth exists on the Left, but proposes that unlike bourgeois myth—which he calls "well-fed, sleek, expansive, [and] garrulous"—leftist myth is aimless and crude: "Whatever it does, there remains about it something stiff and literal, a suggestion of something done to order. ... In fact, what can be more meager than the Stalin* myth? No inventiveness here, and only a clumsy appropriation: the signifier of the myth ... is not varied in the least: it is reduced to a litany."[3]

In other words, Barthes reduces leftist myth to the level of glaring propaganda; he suggests that in proclaiming its ideological messages so boldly, the Left cancels the possibility of any second order of signification, and thereby "abolishes myth."[4]

On one level, it is very difficult for modern readers to excuse Barthes's limited awareness of the Left's potential for making its own myths, especially considering the socialist* mythologies that developed in the second half of the twentieth century in, and about, places such as Cuba, Eastern Europe, and the Soviet Union.* On another, for politically neutral or conservative readers Barthes's argument is not convincing on account of his obvious political bias. Although Barthes claims to highlight history and work against the myths that present themselves as natural and not belonging to any history, he ends up limiting his own analysis to the confrontation between two competing ideologies (bourgeois or capitalist* on the one hand, and left wing or Marxist on the other). By the late 1970s, Barthes did slightly reconsider his position, rejecting the frequently mythological collective messages coming from the May 1968 revolutionaries.

Barthes admitted that it might be possible to also talk about a mythology of the Left, but he never took up its analysis in a systematic way in any of his published work—likely because of his own continued links with leftist politics.

NOTES

1   Roland Barthes, "Preface to the 1970 Edition," in *Mythologies*, trans. Annette Lavers (London: Vintage, 2000), 9.

2   Barthes, *Mythologies*, 145.

3   Barthes, *Mythologies*, 148.

4   Barthes, *Mythologies*, 148.

MODULE 8
PLACE IN THE AUTHOR'S WORK

KEY POINTS

- *Mythologies* was not Barthes's first book, but it finally brought him a wide readership. When it appeared, it was hotly debated by left-wing and right-wing commentators.

- *Mythologies* was the start of Barthes's lifelong focus on the analysis of the hidden meanings of mass media and popular culture. The book inspired other artistic productions (film and fiction writing) that also examined the hidden messages of everyday things.

- Barthes was both fascinated and disgusted by the advertising industry; his semiotic* methods ruthlessly exposed its deeper messages, but at the same time he was willing to help refine their sales strategies.

Positioning

Roland Barthes's *Mythologies* belongs to his journalistic period, in which the bulk of his intellectual work was dedicated to writing for a number of literary magazines. Although most of the essays had already appeared in *Les Lettres nouvelles*, their publication as a book brought a broader readership, and got widespread attention in the press. At this point in his career, Barthes had already published two books, *Writing Degree Zero* (1954) and *Michelet* (1954). But *Mythologies* captured the tense political climate of the 1950s, creating a considerable debate between left-leaning and right-wing commentators.

While the Right was unanimously hostile towards *Mythologies*, the Left was impressed by its social and political critique, and became interested in Barthes for the first time. *Mythologies* was therefore

> ❝ Barthes decided that the postscript would be a theoretical essay, 'Myth Today' … This essay marks his entrance into the semiological order, just as one would enter a religious order. ❞
>
> Louis-Jean Calvet, *Roland Barthes: A Biography*

extremely important to his career, launching debates about Barthes the intellectual, as well as about the relationship between cultural practice, theory, and politics that would come to define the poststructuralist* movement (a philosophical current that questioned the very possibility of any objective, "true" analysis of culture at all).

Although Barthes employed a new terminology in *Mythologies*, he was reshaping ideas he had already explored in *Writing Degree Zero*. For instance, both texts concentrate on demystifying the codes of bourgeois* culture and there is a close parallel between the texts' concepts of signification* (the process of conveying meaning through signs*) and denotation* (the explicit, direct, meaning of things such as words).

In the earlier book, Barthes examined the links between an author's biography and the conditions of writing, arguing that once writers commit to language, they are caught up in established sets of literary signs—or myths. For this reason, Barthes advocated the search for a language that is as yet unmarked by the process of signification, or which works at a level before it; in other words, writing from a degree zero. Here, Barthes is getting at a problem always present in writing: the impossibility of an author taking him or herself out of the enclosure of culture in which they operate.

Integration

It is possible to divide Barthes's work broadly into two phases: an early, structuralist* phase, and a later, poststructuralist one. If structuralists argued that communication could be understood through the study of underlying formal rules, looking at culturally significant opposites such as "day/night" and "dead/alive," poststructuralists ended this insistence, emphasizing, instead, the instability of meaning. This shift means that, for poststructuralist theory, a written text's *reader*, rather than its *writer*, takes on chief importance—as Barthes observes in his groundbreaking essay "The Death of the Author" (1967).

In this context, the author's intended meaning (which, on account of being unstable, is impossible to really know) loses its central position. In its place are the variety of meanings a reader can draw from a text.

Barthes's work in each phase saw enough changes to suggest that he was never really comfortable committing fully to any school of thought. While *Mythologies* belongs to his structuralist phase, its fragmentary construction made up of essays differs a lot from his more systematic and theoretically orientated texts such as *Elements of Semiology* (1967). This points to a wider problem of trying to put distinct labels on his work, or putting his different writings into clear categories. Barthes made significant contributions to the fields of semiotics, literary criticism, linguistics,* and the theory of photography, but much of his work crosses established lines and defies clear classification.

Furthermore, one of the biggest obstacles in writing about Barthes's work as a whole is the disabling power of his criticisms of his own writings. Barthes refused to be tied down by his own achievements and had a tendency to abandon intellectual projects once they were set in motion. He criticized his earlier work sharply, and *Mythologies* was no different. It quickly became a historical piece for Barthes, and its demystifications looked, in his eyes, like overly predictable assessments of culture. That said, *Mythologies* contained the early stages of a preoccupation that Barthes explored throughout his entire career: contextualizing the practice of writing and communication in culture.

Mythologies introduced Marxist* themes and elements of structuralism to the analysis of modern French culture. It was written during a period of social and political turmoil in France, and was aimed at left-wing intellectuals who would have understood the need for establishing a critical dialogue over consumer culture. Prior to the writing of the essays, Barthes had become interested in theoretical Marxism while recovering from a second bout of tuberculosis. The essays assume a familiarity with Marx's analysis of power and ideology in capitalist* societies.

Mythologies helped form the public image of Barthes as a Marxist thinker with a semiologist's critical vision of society. His view of society was becoming part of public discourse. As his biographer Louis-Jean Calvet notes, by the mid-1960s Barthes's ideas were common currency, and were being translated to film by Jean-Luc Godard,* who in *La Femme mariée* (1964) created a montage of little mythologies relating to female alienation—the feeling of being isolated—and to literature by the experimental writer Georges Perec,* who in his novel *Les Choses* (1965) paints a picture of a petit-bourgeois* couple in the making, as if they were characters taken straight out of *Mythologies*.[1]

Although *Mythologies* was sharply critical of French society, Barthes really was part of the spirit of the times. His critiques of advertising even captured the attention of advertising companies, and Barthes was asked to offer seminars to the advertising industry. In an odd reversal of fate, readings from *Mythologies* gradually started being promoted by professional advertisers—the very producers of mass culture that Barthes had set out to critique. In fact, a few years after demystifying the semiology of advertisements for the new car from Citroën (a leading French automobile manufacturer), Barthes accepted an offer to analyze the new advertising strategy of its chief rival, Renault.

Significance

These examples show the immediate influence of Barthes's work. Barthes's writing was always in perpetual production, moving with the times so as not to be contained by any single idea or period. In addition, Barthes was remarkably open to embracing contradictions in his own work. The fact that he accepted a contract to apply his critical ideas to improving car sales points to how he was drawn to consumer culture as much as he was disgusted by it. This also demonstrates how the industry was, in turn, fascinated with Barthes's ideas. The advertising industry was still being built up in the 1950s and Barthes's thinking had a profound impact on its development. *Mythologies* emphasized the importance of critical analysis; advertisers then incorporated, adapted, and extended the results into their own practice to improve commercial strategies. This cross-fertilization perhaps did not clash with Barthes's principles; after all he stressed the importance of constantly questioning basic assumptions so as to be able to look newly and differently at daily French life and better understand new trends and changes in human behavior.

NOTES

1   Louis-Jean Calvet, *Roland Barthes: A Biography*, trans. Sarah Wykes (Cambridge: Polity Press, 1994), 141.

SECTION 3
IMPACT

MODULE 9
THE FIRST RESPONSES

KEY POINTS

- Reactions to the publication of *Mythologies* typically depended on the political orientation of the reviewer, with left-wing publications praising it and right-wing ones panning it. It was also attacked for being sloppy in its use of political and linguistic* theories.

- Once finished, Barthes quickly lost interest in the *Mythologies* project, arguing that the simple critique of signs* was no longer sufficient.

- Barthes enjoyed the status of an irreverent outsider in French intellectual circles.

Criticism

From its publication, Roland Barthes's *Mythologies* prompted sharply different reactions. While the philosophy section of *Le Monde* reviewed the book positively, the right-leaning *Rivarol* and *L'Écho du centre* both criticized Barthes's "progressive idiocies,"[1] and described *Mythologies* as "part interpretative delirium and part pedantic jargon."[2] The criticism it drew at first seemed to depend on the political leaning of individual commentators, but three basic issues quickly arose: Barthes's semiological* approach, his weak political vocabulary, and his approach to criticism which condemned but did not offer alternatives.

The French linguistics professor Georges Mounin* severely criticized Barthes's approach to semiological analysis. In *Introduction à la Sémiologie* (1970)[3] Mounin claimed that Barthes's use of linguistic terms showed a degree of confusion. Mounin argued that Barthes took liberties with the principles of the highly influential linguist

> **"** In *Roland Barthes*, he speaks of 1971 as the year
> in which the phrase 'bourgeois ideology' had gone
> considerably sour and was beginning to 'fatigue.' I am
> suggesting that the problem was already apparent in
> *Mythologies*. If Barthes had not reached the point of
> emotional revulsion from Marxist cliché ... 'bourgeois
> ideology' was nevertheless extremely vulnerable even
> then as an explanatory term. **"**
>
> Eugene Goodheart, *The Skeptic Disposition in Contemporary Criticism*

Ferdinand de Saussure,* setting up a semiology of signification* in a petit-bourgeois* cultural context, rather than a general semiology of linguistic communication. In other words, Mounin stated that Barthes misused Saussure's concept of the sign, giving it a sense so broad that it could include anything that carried meaning. Barthes investigated the hidden elements of social signification and, for this reason, Mounin thought it more appropriate to speak of the collection as a work of social psychology than of semiology.

Barthes famously engaged in a public dispute with the literature scholar Raymond Picard,* who took exception to Barthes's arbitrary and personal approach to classic French literature. Similarly, Barthes's political vocabulary was also criticized for not following any defined political system. In *Mythologies* Barthes took many terms from classical Marxism,* but it is not clear if these simply provided convenient categories through which to attack the petit-bourgeois class.

This attack was based on the idea of myth as a petit-bourgeois system of signification (the process by which a signifier* and a signified* together make a sign and transmit *meaning*) that creates a false consciousness* among wage earners—a Marxist concept that refers to the ways in which members of the dominant class in society control the rest of society through ideological and institutional deceit.

But what seems to be entirely missing from *Mythologies* is an analysis of the political motivations behind this ideological construction. Barthes treated the bourgeoisie* as a fixed object, rather than as dynamic social grouping. For this reason, his analysis is lacking in psychological complexity. Furthermore, when Barthes proposed that myth is necessary for false consciousness, he implied that there is truth outside of myth and ideology. Yet he did nothing to clarify or expand on this proposition. *Mythologies* was also criticized for being a project of negative criticism: it attacked one system but did not offer any practical alternatives.

Author's Response

Barthes's most immediate response can be found in his preface to the 1970 edition of *Mythologies*. He responded to the various criticisms leveled at *Mythologies* by explaining that its message should be seen as being subject to constant change. The book's theoretical framework, he explains, being an ideological critique of the language of mass culture and an analysis of this language, could "no longer today be maintained unchanged … Not because what brought them about has now disappeared, but because ideological criticism … [and] semiological analysis … [have] developed, become more precise, complicated and differentiated."[4]

Barthes did not believe that *Mythologies* could be revised and brought up to date. He reasoned that undertaking a revision of the book would require creating an entire new theoretical system, since the system supporting *Mythologies* could only be persuasive if was historically specific: "I could not … write a new series of mythologies in the form presented here, which belongs to the past."[5]

This relates to a wider concern: how any violation of convention eventually becomes part of the norm. Throughout the 1970s, Barthes questioned his earlier work on mythologies and took a slightly mocking tone with regards to it. In his essay "Change the Object

Itself" (1971), he observed that condemning myths was no longer sufficient, noting that the act of demystification of mass culture had itself "become in some sort mythical."[6] Indeed, denouncing the bourgeoisie through the identification of its ideology had become a common practice by the 1970s. In light of this, Barthes revised his thinking, proposing that instead of decoding signs, the aim should be to get rid of the sign altogether, since "it is no longer the myths which need to be unmasked … it is the sign itself which must be shaken; the problem is … to fissure the very representation of meaning … not to change or purify the symbols, but to change the symbolic itself."[7]

Conflict and Consensus

Barthes's revisions appear to be motivated more by a sense that the method of analysis put forward in *Mythologies* is constantly changing, rather than by the criticisms leveled against it. His revisions show a degree of playfulness and irony that reflect his fascination with everyday myths and second-order levels of signification. They suggest that he never lost his interest: he just insisted on the development of an updated and appropriate method of analysis for a new—and entirely different—network of myths.

Barthes had a tendency to abandon projects once they flourished, promptly moving on to new things. His study of myths was no different and Barthes was criticized for his lack of perseverance. He responded to this by demystifying his previous work and interests by way of mocking them, so these could not themselves become myths of the type he had critiqued.

From a present-day perspective, it looks as if Barthes enjoyed the position of the irreverent outsider who took great joy in provoking trivial disputes within French intellectual circles. His opinions can appear inconsistent and superficial, chosen simply to ruffle the feathers of established thinkers, rather than to follow a consistent political or analytical approach. As a result, later debate on *Mythologies* has centered on its status as a text written by an outsider.

NOTES

1 *Rivarol*, March 28, 1957. Quoted in Louis-Jean Calvet, *Roland Barthes: A Biography*, trans. Sarah Wykes (Cambridge: Polity Press, 1994), 126.

2 *L'Écho du centre*, March 31, 1957. Quoted in Calvet, *Roland Barthes*, 126.

3 Georges Mounin, *Introduction à la Sémiologie* (Paris: Minuit, 1970).

4 Roland Barthes, "Preface to the 1970 Edition," in *Mythologies*, trans. Annette Lavers (London: Vintage, 2000), 9.

5 Barthes, "Preface," 9.

6 Roland Barthes, "Change the Object Itself," in *Image, Music, Text*, trans. Stephen Heath (London: Fontana, 1977), 166.

7 Barthes, "Change the Object Itself," 167.

MODULE 10
THE EVOLVING DEBATE

KEY POINTS

- *Mythologies* changed the way popular culture was understood as a legitimate object of intellectual analysis.

- The discipline of cultural studies and the intellectual institution of postmodernism* drew heavily on the principles laid out in *Mythologies*.

- Popular cultural commentators have taken up the principles of *Mythologies* to critique the media and popular culture.

Uses and Problems

Before the publication of Roland Barthes's *Mythologies*, academics treated popular culture as a little brother to a high-minded idea of culture. Barthes's decision to focus on the common objects of mass culture instead of works that were traditionally considered culturally valuable—such as literature or art—helped begin a change in the way popular culture was understood. *Mythologies* acted out a transitional stage in the development of the idea of culture: the historical moment when popular culture began to be valued as a legitimate object of analysis by scholars.

Despite the emphasis on popular culture that he helped promote, Barthes was unsure about its merits. *Mythologies* captures the uncomfortable coexistence of the contempt for mass culture that characterized modernism* (a cultural movement that challenged the traditional forms still used in the early twentieth century) with a newer postmodern fascination with popular culture. Barthes does not offer much aesthetic* appreciation of the objects of his analysis. He is not interested in judging appearances, in other words. Instead, he deals

> 66 The assumption of a universal human condition—
> across time, across cultures—encourages passivity: if this
> is our fate, if this is our nature, then there is no reason
> to try to change things. But, as Barthes counters, even if
> we are all born, live, and die, we don't always do so in
> equivalent ways and we don't necessarily have to do so
> in the ways ... society has tried to determine for us. 99
>
> Dana Polan, "Roland Barthes's *Mythologies*: A Breakthrough Contribution
> to the Study of Mass Culture"

with popular culture from a detached and often ironic position.

This points to how his project does not end with the analysis of popular culture, but with the development of a new mode of literary and philosophical production founded on theoretical principles of analysis. So it was that in *Mythologies* Barthes worked out a linguistic* model of analysis of popular culture that he connected to a Marxist* sociopolitical criticism of the petite bourgeoisie.* By doing so, he defined cultural criticism as a politically progressive act. This was a key reversal, turning the producers of culture—be it makers of wine, images, or films—into passive carriers of a dominant ideology,* and their commentators—the critics, analysts, and theorists—into the active agents in a progressive cultural politics.

In this way, *Mythologies* gave the production of cultural criticism a new importance and recognition among generations of writers, academics, and students, making criticism as important as the production of the culture itself. The ever-growing popularity of courses geared around criticism in literature and philosophy departments at universities across Europe and North America testifies to one of the work's most important evolutionary effects.

Schools of Thought

Roland Barthes's *Mythologies* is not carried forward by any one school of thought. Instead, it has exerted its influence by inspiring a pedagogical shift, changing the way we can teach, learn, and think about popular culture. The work's legacy can be seen in the development of cultural studies as an academic discipline and, perhaps more significantly, in its shaping of the intellectual character of postmodernism. Here, it "[opened] up the space of postmodernism's valorization and reinvigoration of the popular."[1]

Postmodern critics and practitioners—such as artists and writers— have identified with Barthes's detached and ironic take on mass culture. In *Brecht and Method* (1998), the cultural theorist Fredric Jameson* links Barthes's satirical approach to Bertolt Brecht's* famous *estrangement effect,** in which Brecht looked to jolt theater audiences into a more critical and less emotional involvement with his plays through reminders that what they were watching was staged and not real. Jameson proposes that Barthes's critical detachment from popular culture provides a "textbook 'application' of [Brecht's] method to a range of social and cultural phenomena."[2] For Jameson, this kind of detachment works as a useful interruption to the continuity of the signifying* process by which the signs of popular culture transmit meaning.

Jameson identifies Barthes's detachment as the basis for postmodernist criticism: by freeing themselves from mass culture, postmodern critics are able to develop a critical stance towards its images by disrupting their communication of messages that claim to be natural and universal.

The British novelist Angela Carter alluded to Barthes's influence by stating that her work also belonged to the "demythologizing business."[3] Carter explained that her writing sought to expose the ideologies hidden behind the fictions in our society, in order to rescue our lives from the "extraordinary lies designed to make people unfree."[4] Like *Mythologies,* her writing targeted the "configurations of imagery in our society" that support and communicate unexamined beliefs, or the "ideas, images, stories that we tend to take on trust without thinking what they really mean."[5] For Jameson and Carter, the impulse to challenge audiences to think rather than accept given meanings is a key feature of postmodern creative practice. To blindly accept historical myths about our society and relations is to lose sight of the material conditions of life and the reasons for seeking political change.

In Current Scholarship

Roland Barthes's *Mythologies* had a deep impact on several major intellectual figures in the late twentieth century, including thinkers such as Susan Sontag,* Julia Kristeva,* Paul de Man,* and Jean Baudrillard.* Furthermore, many of Barthes's wider ideas—such as the reader's participation in the authorship of a text—have had a huge impact on modern literary theory. It is difficult, however, to identify individual scholars that can be considered devoted followers of Barthes's ideas in *Mythologies.* While the text's influence can be felt in the work of literary theorists, cultural historians, media analysts, and even theologians (people engaged in the systematic study of religious texts), it is usually as a pioneering reference tool for carrying out a literary reading of mass culture, rather than as an ongoing academic project.

Followers of the ideas that Barthes laid out in *Mythologies* can also be found outside academia in the world of journalism, where cultural commentators indirectly follow his approach by exposing the mythological messages contained in the language of the media, politics, and advertising. Although the study of myth has undergone a significant shift in emphasis and structure in the era of electronic media, the work of popular cultural critics such as the satirical British writer and television producer Charlie Brooker* shows how the grammar of online sharing platforms follows a new kind of mythology that shares cultural codes through virtual groupings. In this sense, *Mythologies* has come full circle, taking a step beyond academia and into the world of popular media that originally produced it.

NOTES

1 Marianne DeKoven, *Utopia Limited: The Sixties and the Emergence of the Postmodern* (Durham, N.C.: Duke University Press, 2004), 60.

2 Fredric Jameson, *Brecht and Method* (London: Verso, 2000), 173.

3 Angela Carter, "Notes from the Front Line," in *Shaking a Leg: Collected Writings* (New York: Penguin, 1998), 38.

4 Carter, "Notes," 38.

5 Angela Carter, interview by Anna Katsavos, "A Conversation with Angela Carter," *The Review of Contemporary Fiction* 14, no. 3 (1994): 11–12.

MODULE 11
IMPACT AND INFLUENCE TODAY

KEY POINTS

- The content of mass culture has changed, but *Mythologies* remains as fresh and important as ever.

- Barthes's model of semiotic* analysis has become a resource for understanding popular culture and mass media, even as they change radically in today's digital world.

- Contemporary scholars continue to discuss present-day myths using Barthes's approach.

Position

For a collection of essays dedicated to analyzing pop culture almost six decades old, Roland Barthes's *Mythologies* feels surprisingly fresh. Many of Barthes's insights are as true for contemporary culture as they were for postwar France. If Barthes was writing during the infancy of mass culture, we are now living through its maturity in the age of digital network technologies, globalization,* and continual multimedia advertising. Although these developments are far removed from the practice at the time Barthes was writing, his semiotic model (that is, his model of society's sign* and symbols) occupies a central place in the analysis of the images of mass culture. The spread of pop culture and digital media has brought renewed freshness to the debate, and Barthes's principal message—that everything means something—remains as powerful and valid as it ever was.

In a footnote to the concluding essay of *Mythologies*, Roland Barthes asks: "In a single day, how many really non-signifying fields do we cross? Very few, sometimes none. Here I am, before the sea … on the beach, what material for semiology! Flags, slogans, signals, sign-

> ❝ A recent example of the plausibility of the Barthesian thesis is the *Absolut Vodka* campaign ... which ... went so far as to imbue its product with the spiritual qualities that are perceived to be so lacking in the hubris of modern secular societies ... a bottle shown with a halo and the caption *Absolut Perfection* ... a winged bottle with the caption *Absolut Heaven*; and ... a bottle held by ... a medieval knight with the caption *Absolut Grail*. ... The overall message of the campaign was rather transparent—spirituality could be obtained by imbibing the vodka. ❞
>
> Ron Beasley and Marcel Danesi, *Persuasive Signs: The Semiotics of Advertising*

boards, clothes, suntan even, which are so many messages to me."[1] Over the past 50 years this landscape has intensified dramatically and today all aspects of our lives are surrounded by slogans. *Mythologies* has been absorbed so fully in the current intellectual climate that it is possible to overlook just how prophetic Barthes's vision was. *Mythologies* continues to challenge modern readers by calling attention to how we have not yet outgrown many of the myths he alerted us to.

Interaction

Although the signifiers* (the physical form of a sign, such as an image, or a printed word) may have changed, it is difficult not to think of Barthes in a huge number of modern contexts.

In politics, it would be easy to find an image of a present-day politician gazing longingly into the distance to insert into Barthes's essay "Photography and Electoral Appeal." Indeed, the attention paid to the construction of favorable political images in campaigns has perhaps even intensified, suggesting that we are still persuaded by the myth of a leader with clear vision and steely determination, and caught in the myth's idiocy. Similarly, Barthes's essay "Operation Margarine" can be read as an early model for the "I Can't Believe It's Not Butter!"* marketing campaign.

In order to increase the appeal of brands—be they a political leader or a margarine—politicians and advertising companies have entire departments dedicated to researching the codes of meaning that define the consumer marketplace. In an unexpected reversal of Barthes's original purpose, semiotic brand analysis is now a vital part of marketing strategy and signals a key change: brand analysts now work with the semiotic tools provided to them by Barthes in order to shape advertising codes and symbols in even more cynical and complex ways. Against this backdrop, Barthes challenges scholars to find new and intelligent ways to think and write through present-day myths, continuing to reveal the structures at work rather than brushing them off with trivial anti-populist criticism.

The Continuing Debate

There are plenty of thinkers across a wide range of debates engaged in decoding present-day myths. As if to confirm the lasting importance of Barthes's ideas as a genuine tool for analysis, the complete *Mythologies* was translated into English for the first time in 2013, 56 years after its original publication. Furthermore, a recent collection edited by media theorists Julian McDougall and Pete Bennett looks to refresh Barthes's text by re-imagining it in a contemporary context. The essays in *Barthes's Mythologies Today: Readings of Contemporary Culture* (2013) set out to question what constitutes myth today. The collection tests the "endurance of mythology as an interpretative regime," asking its contributors to engage with modern culture through Barthes.[2]

Each essay asks questions of the dominant ideological models that are behind modern culture, and follows Barthes's critical approach in looking at different aspects of contemporary culture. Today, these ideological models can be seen in widespread myths that are accepted at face value, such as fair trade commerce, the concept of education as salvation, or the search for unique talent. For instance, television shows such as *The X Factor** absorb, distort, and transform the music industry for entertainment. In his essay "The X Factor," the British media scholar Tim Wall proposes that the quest for the un–definable x–factor is mythical and semiological: it is the commercialization of a fantasy of talent, of ideas of mentoring, and of the democratic participation of audiences. Wall proposes that even though present-day consumers can see through this process, they continue to engage with it, accepting the artifice inherent to the show as real. Furthermore, the illusion of audience participation fosters an unfruitful kind of agency that raises the question of whether contemporary consumers have enough power to influence markets, or whether they are being taken advantage of with even deeper and more sophisticated levels of manipulation.

As myths continue to have a powerful influence on society, modern re-workings of *Mythologies* bring Barthes's ideas to modern settings in order to update his message of awakening to the illusions that surround us. Our times make necessary the development of new methods to decode modern mythologies, and Barthes's principles of myth serve as a valuable companion to modern concerns.

NOTES

1   Roland Barthes, *Mythologies*, trans. Annette Lavers (London: Vintage, 2000), 112.

2   Julian McDougall, "Fables of Reconstruction," in *Barthes's* Mythologies *Today: Readings of Contemporary Culture*, ed. Pete Bennett and Julian McDougall (New York: Routledge, 2013), 7.

MODULE 12
WHERE NEXT?

KEY POINTS

- *Mythologies* shows the need to analyze and critique all cultural messages, including its own.

- Barthes's own methods must be used to update his presentation of consumers as passively taking in culture; in the digital age consumers participate in the production of culture through activities like writing blogs or uploading videos, and the lines between producers and consumers of culture are blurring.

- *Mythologies* remains a fertile text for questioning the origins and uses of cultural signification* (that is, roughly, the process by which meaning is transmitted through signs* in a culture), and for understanding Barthes as an innovative literary writer.

Potential

What place does Roland Barthes's *Mythologies* occupy in our lives today? *Mythologies* works as a mode of signification: a way of making meaning by disclosing and interpreting the myths that surround us in our daily lives. This approach holds the potential to continually be renewed in relation to new social and cultural landscapes. Once it has been accepted that there is no such thing as an innocent message, new systems for deciphering myths can be developed to read future changes in culture, building on a recognition of changing signifying contexts as well as an awareness of their status as mythological. Indeed, *Mythologies* will continue to stimulate debate by allowing itself to be read on its own terms: as a text containing a network of established relationships

> ❝ What is Barthes today? Barthes is a form of speech, a mode of signification. To earn the qualifier 'Barthesian' … is to be defined not by object or material but by a signifying consciousness. Barthes, like 'myth,' is semi-ological. He wouldn't have wanted it any other way. ❞
>
> Pete Bennett, "Barthes' Myth Today"

and classifications that themselves require subverting. Thanks to Barthes, we now have more critical tools at our disposal; indeed, the approach the text promotes must in turn be used on itself in order to point out its own constructed nature. This self-awareness sets an agenda for the continuation of a process of thinking, writing, and demystifying culture.

One important reason for continuing to renew and update Barthes's project in the future is the instability of a uniform understanding of the media. Although the current media landscape contains elements of the model outlined by Barthes, the distribution of culture works in much more varied and hybrid ways. Barthes's hierarchical distinction between producers and consumers of mass culture has become blurred in the digital age, and it is likely that in the future it will become increasingly difficult to talk of consumers as a clearly defined body. Cultural production today is full of fresh contradictions and for this reason *Mythologies* will remain a key reference point. Even though the world Barthes wrote about is being overturned, his reflections maintain their impact precisely because they point to the importance of continuing to develop appropriate types of analysis: "[No] denunciation without an appropriate method of detailed analysis."[1] The fact that *Mythologies* remains challenging is a sign that Barthes tried to avoid letting it be caught up in the system it set out to condemn and undermine.

Future Directions

One area in which the text's core ideas may be further developed is in relation to digital technology. The Internet, in particular, will continue to contribute greatly to destroying the figure of the naive consumer of signs sketched out by Barthes. Instead of just passively consuming pop culture, consumers today participate directly in the creation of culture by reacting to it in real time, volunteering comments and analysis through interactive platforms such as blogs, media comment sections, video responses, and social media sites.

The users of these platforms will harness the social and political potential hinted at in *Mythologies*. In many ways, the platforms function as non-professional forums for decoding myths, challenging Barthes's portrayal of consumers of mass culture as uncritical victims of deception. Far from being routinely duped, present-day consumers are more aware of the logic of advertising and politics than Barthes expected, and the explosion of the amateur critique of mass culture appears to threaten to neutralize his ideas. This form of critique is, however, very much along the lines that Barthes put forward; the examination of everything follows closely in his spirit of inquiry.

This process of criticism is set to be a vital part of culture in the future. The demystification of culture will be as pervasive as the creation of culture, and is becoming as interesting as the object of criticism itself. Whereas Barthes looked at pop culture from outside, in the intellectual environment developing today, with loose boundaries between producers and consumers of culture, criticism and creativity will join together.

Summary

Mythologies is likely to remain a living and influential text because it will always function as a guide to help readers decode the deeper messages or myths of culture, rather than simply as a manual providing a definitive decoding. While Barthes's warning that it is dangerous to reduce things to universals remains a smart observation, he did not work out a complete theory of signification. He does not, for instance, settle why some basic human yearnings—for justice, for idols, for nationhood—become effortlessly attached to the ordinary objects of daily life: wine, detergents, toys, wrestling matches. This question remains open and challenging; students can look to *Mythologies* for the useful frame of reference the work offers for tackling it new time periods. In addition, even though *Mythologies* rapidly became outdated for Barthes, its essays do not read as mere examples of an old-fashioned mode of cultural criticism: each individual essay remains persuasive in a way that ensures that the collection can be read as more than a relic of its own time.

The broad display of cultural interests contained in *Mythologies*— as in Barthes's wider work—makes it difficult to define Barthes's project. For students of literature, this opens up the possibility of thinking of him first and foremost as a writer. *Mythologies* is an experiment in writing; in the pursuit of a way of chronicling the small and trivial incidents from daily life that capture our attention but do not add up to the status of events. Barthes is an anthropologist of modern life, and *Mythologies* began a new form of literary production that eventually led to the now widespread type of blog journalism: cultural criticism. *Mythologies* is ground-breaking because its guiding impulse and critical edge can be taken forward endlessly, encouraging a curious spirit of inquiry and sensitive feeling for everything—no matter how trivial—that the world around us contains.

NOTES

1   Roland Barthes, *Mythologies*, trans. Annette Lavers (London: Vintage, 2000), 9.

GLOSSARY

GLOSSARY OF TERMS

Aesthetics: a branch of philosophy concerned with the evaluation of beauty.

Algerian War: a conflict, also called the Algerian War of Independence (1954–62), in which the National Liberation Front began a war for Algerian independence from France, seeking recognition at the United Nations to establish a sovereign Algerian state.

Baccalauréat: the examination at the end of secondary education in France that regulates university entrance.

Bourgeoisie: a social order made up of the middle classes. In social and political theory, the term is used by Marxists to describe the social class that monopolizes the benefits of modernization to the detriment of the proletariat.

Capitalism: an economic system dominant in the Western world since the break-up of feudalism, in which most of the means of production are privately owned and production is guided and income distributed through the operation of markets.

Cold War (1947–91): period of high political tension from roughly 1947 to 1991 between a group of countries known as the Western bloc, which included the United States and its European allies, and the Eastern bloc, a group of nations including the Soviet Union and its European allies.

Commodity fetishism: a theory advanced by the German economist and political theorist Karl Marx, in which he proposes that people in capitalist societies do not desire products for their intrinsic qualities but as symbols of the social values they represent, such as how much they cost or what demand for the product exists. Marx distinguishes between the exchange value (the price a commodity commands on the market) and the use value (the practical value the commodity provides) of commodities.

Communism: a political ideology that relies on the state ownership of the means of production, the collectivization of labor, and the abolition of social class.

Connotation: in semiotics, "connotation" refers to the associated or secondary meaning of words or other phenomena in addition to their explicit or primary meaning.

Critical theory: a philosophical approach that seeks to combine philosophy with social analysis. In a more narrow sense it also designates the Frankfurt School of philosophers and social theorists.

Cultural turn: movement in the humanities and social sciences during the 1970s that shifted the focus of debates in these disciplines towards the study of culture in all its forms. It is commonly associated with the rise of postmodernism in its considerations of the socioeconomic and political dimensions of postmodern culture.

Denotation: in semiotics, "denotation" refers to the explicit or direct meaning of words and other phenomena, as distinguished from the ideas or meanings associated with them.

Estrangement effect: also known as alienation effect. Theatrical term devised by dramatist Bertolt Brecht. In practice it involves using a number of devices in staging and acting that were designed to create a sense of distance between the audience and the characters in the story. Through these techniques he hoped to remind viewers of the artificiality of theatrical performance and encourage a critical, rather than emotional, response to it.

Existentialism: a term used to describe a complex philosophical tradition emerging in the 1930s with many forms and varieties. Broadly, it can be said to focus philosophy on human existence in the world, and on the possibilities available to human beings in the world. Key existential philosophers include Jean-Paul Sartre, Simone de Beauvoir, and Albert Camus.

False consciousness: a Marxist concept that refers to the ways in which members of the dominant class in society control the rest of society through ideological and institutional deceit.

French Revolution: also called the Revolution of 1789, this was a revolutionary movement that shook France between 1787 and 1799, and that changed Europe irrevocably, marking the decline of the power of absolute monarchies and organized religion in favor of democracies and republics.

Globalization: a process of integration and interaction among the governments, peoples, and companies of different countries. The process is fueled by international trade and investment, and propelled by information technology.

Hungarian Revolution of 1956: popular uprising in Hungary in 1956 against the communist government of Hungary and its Soviet-imposed policies. On November 4 the Soviet Union invaded Hungary to stop the revolution.

I Can't Believe it's Not Butter: a butter substitute largely made from vegetable oil, produced by the British-Dutch company Unilever, and largely sold in the Americas and the United Kingdom.

Ideology: a system of beliefs or principles that aspire to explain the world or change it.

Lexicology: the branch of linguistics that is concerned with the form, meaning, and application of words.

Linguistics: the scientific study of language and its structure. Modern linguists focus on how languages operate at any given point in time, researching grammar and meaning, language acquisition, and the structure of communication.

Marxism: Marxism is a worldview and form of socioeconomic inquiry rooted in the economic theory of the nineteenth-century economist and political theorist Karl Marx and the industrialist Friedrich Engels.

May 1968: student revolt in May 1968 against capitalism and traditional bourgeois culture in France, which spread to uprisings in streets, factories, schools, and universities.

Modernism: a cultural movement that came into existence during the mid-to-late nineteenth century, and which had a profound impact on art and thought in Europe and America from roughly 1900. Modernism is best understood as a culture—or a series of ideas, beliefs, and values—that rebelled against Victorian ideals and led to an explosion in creativity in the arts.

Nationalism: an ideology built on the belief that the individual's loyalty to a nation-state is more important than other individual or group interests. In politics it points to the reciprocal identification of the state with the people.

Nazism: a totalitarian political movement led by Adolf Hitler, the head of the Nazi Party, who ruled Germany between 1933 and 1945. Nazism was characterized by its fervent nationalism, dictatorial rule, state control of the economy, military expansion in Europe, and brutal anti-Semitism, which resulted in the systematic extermination of six million Jews during World War II.

Neo-Marxist: a philosophical and economic approach to the analysis of society derived from the theories of Karl Marx but differing from classical Marxism in certain ways that acknowledge the social and technological changes and advancements made since the end of the nineteenth century.

Petite bourgeoisie: the aspirational lower middle classes. Unlike the high bourgeoisie, they do not own the means of production: they are mid-tier workers who are characterized by the desire to identify with this higher social class bourgeoisie through material consumption.

Postmodernism: a movement in the arts emerging after World War II. Postmodernism involves both a continuation as well as a break from the counter-traditional experiments of modernism, which in time had inevitably become conventional. Postmodernism breaks from the elitism of modernist high art by recourse to the models of mass culture in film, television, and architecture.

Poststructuralism: literary and philosophical movement that emerged in France in the 1970s. Poststructuralism seeks to critique the search to find stable meanings, emphasizing instead a number of different viewpoints and interpretations and less emphasis on finding definitive meanings. Writers associated with the movement include Barthes, Julia Kristeva, and Michel Foucault.

Proletariat: the lowest economic and social class in society. In Marxism the term designates a class of wageworkers that are engaged in industrial production, as opposed to simply the poor.

Semioclasm: term referring to the radical goal in semiotics of total destruction of the sign through the elimination of sacred status of certain orders of signification.

Semiotics or semiology: the study of society's symbols and signs, and of how meaning is created and communicated through these signs. Modern semiotics has its origins in the work of Ferdinand de Saussure.

Sign: in linguistics, a sign is the combination of a material signifier (an image or a printed word, for example) and a signified (the meaning it expresses).

Signification: in linguistics, "signification" refers to the process of conveying meaning through linguistic signs. In Saussurian terms, signification is the process that results from the relationship between the signifier and signified.

Signified: in linguistics, this refers to the meaning or idea expressed by a sign. It is a mental concept, distinct from the physical form in which it is expressed.

Signifier: in linguistics it is the physical unit that conveys meaning, such as speech sounds, printed words, or images.

Socialism: a political and economic theory of social organization that advocates that the means of production, distribution, and exchange should be owned or regulated by the community as a whole.

Soviet Union: also known as the Union of Soviet Socialist Republics (USSR), a union that was governed as a single, Marxist-Leninist state with a central capital in Moscow between 1922 and 1991, when it disintegrated into 15 separate countries.

Stalinism: political method associated with Joseph Stalin. Stalinism is characterized by a totalitarian application of a communist ideology.

Structuralism: an intellectual movement of the early twentieth century. It is characterized by the belief that human culture and societies are governed by underlying patterns and forces that interact in a larger system.

Totalitarianism: a form of government that is highly centralized in one ruler who is unrestricted by a constitution or checks and balances.

Tour de France: yearly bicycle race held in France. It is considered to be the most difficult and prestigious bicycle race in the world.

World War I (1914–18): global conflict that began in 1914, pitting the Allies, a group of countries including the United Kingdom, France and Russia, against the Central Powers, which included Germany, Austria-Hungary and the Ottoman Empire. The war ended in 1918 with the defeat of the Central Powers.

World War II (1939–45): the most widespread military conflict in history, resulting in more than 50 million casualties. While the conflict began with Germany's invasion of Poland in 1939, it soon involved all of the major world powers, who gradually formed two military alliances and were eventually joined by a great number vast of the world's nations.

The X Factor: a televised talent show, originally created for British television, now broadcast in many countries around the world.

PEOPLE MENTIONED IN THE TEXT

Theodor W. Adorno (1903–69) was one of the leading philosophers of the Frankfurt School of critical theory. He made significant contributions to the intellectual fields of philosophy, musicology, aesthetics, and sociology.

Jean Baudrillard (1929–2007) was a French philosopher and cultural critic associated with poststructuralism and, in particular, with theories of postmodernism and the mediation of communication. His text *Simulacra and Simulation* (1981) argues that human experience has become one of simulation, where signs and symbols that were thought to represent reality in fact come to stand in for it.

Walter Benjamin (1892–1940) was a German literary critic and essayist associated with the Frankfurt School of social theorists who is regarded as one of the most important intellectual figures of the twentieth century. He is best known for his essay "The Work of Art in the Age of Mechanical Reproduction" (1936).

Bertolt Brecht (1898–1956) was a German poet and playwright who made significant contributions to dramatic theory. His concept of epic theater challenged theatrical conventions by disrupting notions of dramatic illusion in favor of a more politically engaged type of theater.

Charlie Brooker (b. 1971) is an English satirist, columnist, and broadcaster.

Charles de Gaulle (1890–70) was a French military leader, statesman, and writer who became the president of France between 1959 and 1969. His time as president was marked by the student and worker uprisings in 1968.

Paul de Man (1919–83) was a Belgian-born literary critic. He was one of the main proponents of deconstruction.

Sigmund Freud (1856–1939) was an Austrian neurologist and founder of psychoanalysis. He proposed that a system of unconscious drives and repressions determined much of human behavior.

Greta Garbo (1905–90) was a popular Swedish American film star of the 1920s and 1930s. She is known for her portrayals of sultry and moody heroines.

Jean-Luc Godard (b. 1930) is a French film director who rose to prominence as one of the central figures of the new wave filmmaking group in the 1960s. He is best known for his film *Breathless* (1960).

Max Horkheimer (1895–1973) was a German philosopher and cultural critic. His writings influenced the orientation of the Frankfurt School of critical theory and had a lasting influence on subsequent critical thought.

Fredric Jameson (b. 1934) is a preeminent American literary and critical theorist who has published widely on Marxism, poststructuralism, and postmodernism.

Julia Kristeva (b. 1941) is a Bulgarian-French feminist philosopher, psychoanalyst, and literary critic. She is known for her writings in structuralist linguistics, psychoanalysis, and philosophical feminism. Her works include *Woman's Time* (1981), *Powers of Horror* (1982), and *Black Sun* (1992).

Henri Lefebvre (1901–91) was a French philosopher best known for his writing on everyday environments and the nature of space. His work played a critical role in cultural and architectural debates from the 1920s until his death.

Claude Lévi-Strauss (1908–2009) was a French ethnologist and anthropologist. He is frequently cited as the father of modern anthropology.

Karl Marx (1818–83) was a German sociologist, economist, and revolutionary. Along with Friedrich Engels he wrote *The Communist Manifesto*, as well as writing *Das Kapital*, which form the basis of the body of thought known as Marxism.

Marshall McLuhan (1911–80) was a Canadian communications theorist. He is known for his aphorism "the medium is the message," which summarizes his view of the powerful influence of television and electronic media in shaping thought in contemporary society.

Georges Mounin (1910–93) was a French linguist and professor of linguistics and semiology at the University of Aix-en-Provence.

Georges Perec (1936–82) was a French writer known for his novel *A Void* (1969), which was written entirely without using the letter "e"—and *Life: A User's Manual* (1978). He is considered one of the greatest formal innovators of his generation.

Raymond Picard (1917–75) was a French author, prominent professor in literature at the Sorbonne, and Jean Racine scholar.

Pierre Poujade (1920–2003) was a French publisher and politician. He led a controversial right-wing protest movement called Poujadisme in France during the 1950s.

Jean-Paul Sartre (1905–80) was a leading French existential philosopher, writer, and activist. His work relied heavily on the idea that individuals are condemned to be free, and that there is no creator.

Ferdinand de Saussure (1857–1913) was a Swiss linguist whose ideas on structure in language laid the foundation for the linguistic sciences in the twentieth century.

Susan Sontag (1933–2004) was an American intellectual and writer best known for her essays on modern culture. Her work is characterized by approaching a variety of aspects of modern culture philosophically.

Joseph Stalin (1878–1953) was the leader of the Soviet Union from the mid-1920s until his death. He ruthlessly eliminated all opposition to his rule, both inside and outside the Communist Party, which held a monopoly of power until the collapse of the Soviet Union in 1991.

Raymond Williams (1921–88) was a Welsh academic and Marxist critic whose work laid the foundations for cultural studies.

WORKS CITED

WORKS CITED

Adorno, Theodor W., and Max Horkheimer. "The Culture Industry: Enlightenment as Mass Deception." In *Dialectic of Enlightenment*. Translated by John Cumming. London: Verso, 1997.

Barthes, Roland. "Change the Object Itself." In *Image, Music, Text*, 165–9. Translated by Stephen Heath. London: Fontana, 1977.

— — —. *Mythologies*. Translated by Annette Lavers. London: Vintage, 2000.

— — —. "Poujade and the Intellectuals." In *The Eiffel Tower and Other Mythologies*, 127–36. Translated by Richard Howard. London: University of California Press, 1997.

— — —. *Roland Barthes by Roland Barthes*. Translated by Richard Howard. New York: Hill & Wang, 1977.

— — —. *Writing Degree Zero*. Translated by Annette Levers and Colin Smith. New York: Hill & Wang, 2012.

Beasley, Ron, and Marcel Danesi. *Persuasive Signs: The Semiotics of Advertising*. New York: Mouton de Gruyter, 2002.

Benjamin, Walter. "The Work of Art in the Age of Mechanical Reproduction." In *Illuminations*. Edited by Hannah Arendt, translated by Harry Zohn, preface by Leon Wieseltier. New York: Shocken Books, 2007.

Bennett, Pete. "Barthes' Myth Today." In *Barthes's* Mythologies *Today: Readings of Contemporary Culture*, edited by Pete Bennett and Julian McDougall, 143–65. New York: Routledge, 2013.

Calvet, Louis-Jean. *Roland Barthes: A Biography*. Translated by Sarah Wykes. Cambridge: Polity Press, 1994.

Carter, Angela. "Notes from the Front Line." In *Shaking a Leg: Collected Writings*, 36–43. New York: Penguin, 1998.

Chapman, Siobhan, and Christopher Routledge, eds. *Key Thinkers in Linguistics and the Philosophy of Language*. Oxford: Oxford University Press, 2005.

DeKoven, Marianne. *Utopia Limited: The Sixties and the Emergence of the Postmodern*. Durham, N.C.: Duke University Press, 2004.

Denning, Michael. *Culture in the Age of Three Worlds*. London: Verso, 2004.

Eagleton, Terry. *Ideology: An Introduction*. London: Verso, 1991.

Gibian, Peter. "On/Against Mass Culture Theories." In *Mass Culture and Everyday Life*, edited by Peter Gibian, 14–24. Oxford: Routledge, 1997.

Goodheart, Eugene. *The Skeptic Disposition in Contemporary Criticism*. Princeton, N.J.: Princeton University Press, 1984.

Jameson, Fredric. *Brecht and Method*. London: Verso, 2000.

Katsavos, Anna. "A Conversation with Angela Carter." *The Review of Contemporary Fiction* 14, no. 3 (1994): 11–17.

Kelly, Michael. "Demystification: A Dialogue between Barthes and Lefebvre." *Yale French Studies* 98 (2000): 79–97.

Lechte, John. *Fifty Key Contemporary Thinkers: From Structuralism to Postmodernity*. London: Routledge, 1994.

Lefebvre, Henri. *Critique of Everyday Life: The One-Volume Edition*. Translated by John Moore. London: Verso, 2014.

Lévi-Strauss, Claude. "The Structural Study of Myth." *The Journal of American Folklore* 68, no. 270 (1955): 428–44.

McDougall, Julian. "Fables of Reconstruction." In *Barthes's* Mythologies *Today: Readings of Contemporary Culture*, edited by Pete Bennett and Julian McDougall, 3–13. New York: Routledge, 2013.

Moriarty, Michael. *Roland Barthes*. Stanford, CA: Stanford University Press, 1991.

Mounin, Georges. *Introduction à la Sémiologie*. Paris: Minuit, 1970.

Polan, Dana. "Roland Barthes's *Mythologies*: A Breakthrough Contribution to the Study of Mass Culture." In *The Routledge Companion to Global Popular Culture*, edited by Toby Miller. New York: Routledge, 2015.

Ross, Kristin. *Fast Cars, Clean Bodies: Decolonization and the Reordering of French Culture*. Cambridge, MA: MIT Press, 1995.

Scarborough, Milton. *Myth and Modernity: Postcritical Reflections*. Albany: State University of New York, 1994.

THE MACAT LIBRARY
BY DISCIPLINE

AFRICANA STUDIES

Chinua Achebe's *An Image of Africa: Racism in Conrad's Heart of Darkness*
W. E. B. Du Bois's *The Souls of Black Folk*
Zora Neale Huston's *Characteristics of Negro Expression*
Martin Luther King Jr's *Why We Can't Wait*
Toni Morrison's *Playing in the Dark: Whiteness in the American Literary Imagination*

ANTHROPOLOGY

Arjun Appadurai's *Modernity at Large: Cultural Dimensions of Globalisation*
Philippe Ariès's *Centuries of Childhood*
Franz Boas's *Race, Language and Culture*
Kim Chan & Renée Mauborgne's *Blue Ocean Strategy*
Jared Diamond's *Guns, Germs & Steel: the Fate of Human Societies*
Jared Diamond's *Collapse: How Societies Choose to Fail or Survive*
E. E. Evans-Pritchard's *Witchcraft, Oracles and Magic Among the Azande*
James Ferguson's *The Anti-Politics Machine*
Clifford Geertz's *The Interpretation of Cultures*
David Graeber's *Debt: the First 5000 Years*
Karen Ho's *Liquidated: An Ethnography of Wall Street*
Geert Hofstede's *Culture's Consequences: Comparing Values, Behaviors, Institutes and Organizations across Nations*
Claude Lévi-Strauss's *Structural Anthropology*
Jay Macleod's *Ain't No Makin' It: Aspirations and Attainment in a Low-Income Neighborhood*
Saba Mahmood's *The Politics of Piety: The Islamic Revival and the Feminist Subject*
Marcel Mauss's *The Gift*

BUSINESS

Jean Lave & Etienne Wenger's *Situated Learning*
Theodore Levitt's *Marketing Myopia*
Burton G. Malkiel's *A Random Walk Down Wall Street*
Douglas McGregor's *The Human Side of Enterprise*
Michael Porter's *Competitive Strategy: Creating and Sustaining Superior Performance*
John Kotter's *Leading Change*
C. K. Prahalad & Gary Hamel's *The Core Competence of the Corporation*

CRIMINOLOGY

Michelle Alexander's *The New Jim Crow: Mass Incarceration in the Age of Colorblindness*
Michael R. Gottfredson & Travis Hirschi's *A General Theory of Crime*
Richard Herrnstein & Charles A. Murray's *The Bell Curve: Intelligence and Class Structure in American Life*
Elizabeth Loftus's *Eyewitness Testimony*
Jay Macleod's *Ain't No Makin' It: Aspirations and Attainment in a Low-Income Neighborhood*
Philip Zimbardo's *The Lucifer Effect*

ECONOMICS

Janet Abu-Lughod's *Before European Hegemony*
Ha-Joon Chang's *Kicking Away the Ladder*
David Brion Davis's *The Problem of Slavery in the Age of Revolution*
Milton Friedman's *The Role of Monetary Policy*
Milton Friedman's *Capitalism and Freedom*
David Graeber's *Debt: the First 5000 Years*
Friedrich Hayek's *The Road to Serfdom*
Karen Ho's *Liquidated: An Ethnography of Wall Street*

John Maynard Keynes's *The General Theory of Employment, Interest and Money*
Charles P. Kindleberger's *Manias, Panics and Crashes*
Robert Lucas's *Why Doesn't Capital Flow from Rich to Poor Countries?*
Burton G. Malkiel's *A Random Walk Down Wall Street*
Thomas Robert Malthus's *An Essay on the Principle of Population*
Karl Marx's *Capital*
Thomas Piketty's *Capital in the Twenty-First Century*
Amartya Sen's *Development as Freedom*
Adam Smith's *The Wealth of Nations*
Nassim Nicholas Taleb's *The Black Swan: The Impact of the Highly Improbable*
Amos Tversky's & Daniel Kahneman's *Judgment under Uncertainty: Heuristics and Biases*
Mahbub Ul Haq's *Reflections on Human Development*
Max Weber's *The Protestant Ethic and the Spirit of Capitalism*

FEMINISM AND GENDER STUDIES

Judith Butler's *Gender Trouble*
Simone De Beauvoir's *The Second Sex*
Michel Foucault's *History of Sexuality*
Betty Friedan's *The Feminine Mystique*
Saba Mahmood's *The Politics of Piety: The Islamic Revival and the Feminist Subjec*t
Joan Wallach Scott's *Gender and the Politics of History*
Mary Wollstonecraft's *A Vindication of the Rights of Woman*
Virginia Woolf's *A Room of One's Own*

GEOGRAPHY

The Brundtland Report's *Our Common Future*
Rachel Carson's *Silent Spring*
Charles Darwin's *On the Origin of Species*
James Ferguson's *The Anti-Politics Machine*
Jane Jacobs's *The Death and Life of Great American Cities*
James Lovelock's *Gaia: A New Look at Life on Earth*
Amartya Sen's *Development as Freedom*
Mathis Wackernagel & William Rees's *Our Ecological Footprint*

HISTORY

Janet Abu-Lughod's *Before European Hegemony*
Benedict Anderson's *Imagined Communities*
Bernard Bailyn's *The Ideological Origins of the American Revolution*
Hanna Batatu's *The Old Social Classes And The Revolutionary Movements Of Iraq*
Christopher Browning's *Ordinary Men: Reserve Police Batallion 101 and the Final Solution in Poland*
Edmund Burke's *Reflections on the Revolution in France*
William Cronon's *Nature's Metropolis: Chicago And The Great West*
Alfred W. Crosby's *The Columbian Exchange*
Hamid Dabashi's *Iran: A People Interrupted*
David Brion Davis's *The Problem of Slavery in the Age of Revolution*
Nathalie Zemon Davis's *The Return of Martin Guerre*
Jared Diamond's *Guns, Germs & Steel: the Fate of Human Societies*
Frank Dikotter's *Mao's Great Famine*
John W Dower's *War Without Mercy: Race And Power In The Pacific War*
W. E. B. Du Bois's *The Souls of Black Folk*
Richard J. Evans's *In Defence of History*
Lucien Febvre's *The Problem of Unbelief in the 16th Century*
Sheila Fitzpatrick's *Everyday Stalinism*

Eric Foner's *Reconstruction: America's Unfinished Revolution, 1863-1877*
Michel Foucault's *Discipline and Punish*
Michel Foucault's *History of Sexuality*
Francis Fukuyama's *The End of History and the Last Man*
John Lewis Gaddis's *We Now Know: Rethinking Cold War History*
Ernest Gellner's *Nations and Nationalism*
Eugene Genovese's *Roll, Jordan, Roll: The World the Slaves Made*
Carlo Ginzburg's *The Night Battles*
Daniel Goldhagen's *Hitler's Willing Executioners*
Jack Goldstone's *Revolution and Rebellion in the Early Modern World*
Antonio Gramsci's *The Prison Notebooks*
Alexander Hamilton, John Jay & James Madison's *The Federalist Papers*
Christopher Hill's *The World Turned Upside Down*
Carole Hillenbrand's *The Crusades: Islamic Perspectives*
Thomas Hobbes's *Leviathan*
Eric Hobsbawm's *The Age Of Revolution*
John A. Hobson's *Imperialism: A Study*
Albert Hourani's *History of the Arab Peoples*
Samuel P. Huntington's *The Clash of Civilizations and the Remaking of World Order*
C. L. R. James's *The Black Jacobins*
Tony Judt's *Postwar: A History of Europe Since 1945*
Ernst Kantorowicz's *The King's Two Bodies: A Study in Medieval Political Theology*
Paul Kennedy's *The Rise and Fall of the Great Powers*
Ian Kershaw's *The "Hitler Myth": Image and Reality in the Third Reich*
John Maynard Keynes's *The General Theory of Employment, Interest and Money*
Charles P. Kindleberger's *Manias, Panics and Crashes*
Martin Luther King Jr's *Why We Can't Wait*
Henry Kissinger's *World Order: Reflections on the Character of Nations and the Course of History*
Thomas Kuhn's *The Structure of Scientific Revolutions*
Georges Lefebvre's *The Coming of the French Revolution*
John Locke's *Two Treatises of Government*
Niccolò Machiavelli's *The Prince*
Thomas Robert Malthus's *An Essay on the Principle of Population*
Mahmood Mamdani's *Citizen and Subject: Contemporary Africa And The Legacy Of Late Colonialism*
Karl Marx's *Capital*
Stanley Milgram's *Obedience to Authority*
John Stuart Mill's *On Liberty*
Thomas Paine's *Common Sense*
Thomas Paine's *Rights of Man*
Geoffrey Parker's *Global Crisis: War, Climate Change and Catastrophe in the Seventeenth Century*
Jonathan Riley-Smith's *The First Crusade and the Idea of Crusading*
Jean-Jacques Rousseau's *The Social Contract*
Joan Wallach Scott's *Gender and the Politics of History*
Theda Skocpol's *States and Social Revolutions*
Adam Smith's *The Wealth of Nations*
Timothy Snyder's *Bloodlands: Europe Between Hitler and Stalin*
Sun Tzu's *The Art of War*
Keith Thomas's *Religion and the Decline of Magic*
Thucydides's *The History of the Peloponnesian War*
Frederick Jackson Turner's *The Significance of the Frontier in American History*
Odd Arne Westad's *The Global Cold War: Third World Interventions And The Making Of Our Times*

LITERATURE

Chinua Achebe's *An Image of Africa: Racism in Conrad's Heart of Darkness*
Roland Barthes's *Mythologies*
Homi K. Bhabha's *The Location of Culture*
Judith Butler's *Gender Trouble*
Simone De Beauvoir's *The Second Sex*
Ferdinand De Saussure's *Course in General Linguistics*
T. S. Eliot's *The Sacred Wood: Essays on Poetry and Criticism*
Zora Neale Huston's *Characteristics of Negro Expression*
Toni Morrison's *Playing in the Dark: Whiteness in the American Literary Imagination*
Edward Said's *Orientalism*
Gayatri Chakravorty Spivak's *Can the Subaltern Speak?*
Mary Wollstonecraft's *A Vindication of the Rights of Women*
Virginia Woolf's *A Room of One's Own*

PHILOSOPHY

Elizabeth Anscombe's *Modern Moral Philosophy*
Hannah Arendt's *The Human Condition*
Aristotle's *Metaphysics*
Aristotle's *Nicomachean Ethics*
Edmund Gettier's *Is Justified True Belief Knowledge?*
Georg Wilhelm Friedrich Hegel's *Phenomenology of Spirit*
David Hume's *Dialogues Concerning Natural Religion*
David Hume's *The Enquiry for Human Understanding*
Immanuel Kant's *Religion within the Boundaries of Mere Reason*
Immanuel Kant's *Critique of Pure Reason*
Søren Kierkegaard's *The Sickness Unto Death*
Søren Kierkegaard's *Fear and Trembling*
C. S. Lewis's *The Abolition of Man*
Alasdair MacIntyre's *After Virtue*
Marcus Aurelius's *Meditations*
Friedrich Nietzsche's *On the Genealogy of Morality*
Friedrich Nietzsche's *Beyond Good and Evil*
Plato's *Republic*
Plato's *Symposium*
Jean-Jacques Rousseau's *The Social Contract*
Gilbert Ryle's *The Concept of Mind*
Baruch Spinoza's *Ethics*
Sun Tzu's *The Art of War*
Ludwig Wittgenstein's *Philosophical Investigations*

POLITICS

Benedict Anderson's *Imagined Communities*
Aristotle's *Politics*
Bernard Bailyn's *The Ideological Origins of the American Revolution*
Edmund Burke's *Reflections on the Revolution in France*
John C. Calhoun's *A Disquisition on Government*
Ha-Joon Chang's *Kicking Away the Ladder*
Hamid Dabashi's *Iran: A People Interrupted*
Hamid Dabashi's *Theology of Discontent: The Ideological Foundation of the Islamic Revolution in Iran*
Robert Dahl's *Democracy and its Critics*
Robert Dahl's *Who Governs?*
David Brion Davis's *The Problem of Slavery in the Age of Revolution*

Alexis De Tocqueville's *Democracy in America*
James Ferguson's *The Anti-Politics Machine*
Frank Dikotter's *Mao's Great Famine*
Sheila Fitzpatrick's *Everyday Stalinism*
Eric Foner's *Reconstruction: America's Unfinished Revolution, 1863-1877*
Milton Friedman's *Capitalism and Freedom*
Francis Fukuyama's *The End of History and the Last Man*
John Lewis Gaddis's *We Now Know: Rethinking Cold War History*
Ernest Gellner's *Nations and Nationalism*
David Graeber's *Debt: the First 5000 Years*
Antonio Gramsci's *The Prison Notebooks*
Alexander Hamilton, John Jay & James Madison's *The Federalist Papers*
Friedrich Hayek's *The Road to Serfdom*
Christopher Hill's *The World Turned Upside Down*
Thomas Hobbes's *Leviathan*
John A. Hobson's *Imperialism: A Study*
Samuel P. Huntington's *The Clash of Civilizations and the Remaking of World Order*
Tony Judt's *Postwar: A History of Europe Since 1945*
David C. Kang's *China Rising: Peace, Power and Order in East Asia*
Paul Kennedy's *The Rise and Fall of Great Powers*
Robert Keohane's *After Hegemony*
Martin Luther King Jr.'s *Why We Can't Wait*
Henry Kissinger's *World Order: Reflections on the Character of Nations and the Course of History*
John Locke's *Two Treatises of Government*
Niccolò Machiavelli's *The Prince*
Thomas Robert Malthus's *An Essay on the Principle of Population*
Mahmood Mamdani's *Citizen and Subject: Contemporary Africa And The Legacy Of Late Colonialism*
Karl Marx's *Capital*
John Stuart Mill's *On Liberty*
John Stuart Mill's *Utilitarianism*
Hans Morgenthau's *Politics Among Nations*
Thomas Paine's *Common Sense*
Thomas Paine's *Rights of Man*
Thomas Piketty's *Capital in the Twenty-First Century*
Robert D. Putman's *Bowling Alone*
John Rawls's *Theory of Justice*
Jean-Jacques Rousseau's *The Social Contract*
Theda Skocpol's *States and Social Revolutions*
Adam Smith's *The Wealth of Nations*
Sun Tzu's *The Art of War*
Henry David Thoreau's *Civil Disobedience*
Thucydides's *The History of the Peloponnesian War*
Kenneth Waltz's *Theory of International Politics*
Max Weber's *Politics as a Vocation*
Odd Arne Westad's *The Global Cold War: Third World Interventions And The Making Of Our Times*

POSTCOLONIAL STUDIES

Roland Barthes's *Mythologies*
Frantz Fanon's *Black Skin, White Masks*
Homi K. Bhabha's *The Location of Culture*
Gustavo Gutiérrez's *A Theology of Liberation*
Edward Said's *Orientalism*
Gayatri Chakravorty Spivak's *Can the Subaltern Speak?*

PSYCHOLOGY

Gordon Allport's *The Nature of Prejudice*
Alan Baddeley & Graham Hitch's *Aggression: A Social Learning Analysis*
Albert Bandura's *Aggression: A Social Learning Analysis*
Leon Festinger's *A Theory of Cognitive Dissonance*
Sigmund Freud's *The Interpretation of Dreams*
Betty Friedan's *The Feminine Mystique*
Michael R. Gottfredson & Travis Hirschi's *A General Theory of Crime*
Eric Hoffer's *The True Believer: Thoughts on the Nature of Mass Movements*
William James's *Principles of Psychology*
Elizabeth Loftus's *Eyewitness Testimony*
A. H. Maslow's *A Theory of Human Motivation*
Stanley Milgram's *Obedience to Authority*
Steven Pinker's *The Better Angels of Our Nature*
Oliver Sacks's *The Man Who Mistook His Wife For a Hat*
Richard Thaler & Cass Sunstein's *Nudge: Improving Decisions About Health, Wealth and Happiness*
Amos Tversky's *Judgment under Uncertainty: Heuristics and Biases*
Philip Zimbardo's *The Lucifer Effect*

SCIENCE

Rachel Carson's *Silent Spring*
William Cronon's *Nature's Metropolis: Chicago And The Great West*
Alfred W. Crosby's *The Columbian Exchange*
Charles Darwin's *On the Origin of Species*
Richard Dawkin's *The Selfish Gene*
Thomas Kuhn's *The Structure of Scientific Revolutions*
Geoffrey Parker's *Global Crisis: War, Climate Change and Catastrophe in the Seventeenth Century*
Mathis Wackernagel & William Rees's *Our Ecological Footprint*

SOCIOLOGY

Michelle Alexander's *The New Jim Crow: Mass Incarceration in the Age of Colorblindness*
Gordon Allport's *The Nature of Prejudice*
Albert Bandura's *Aggression: A Social Learning Analysis*
Hanna Batatu's *The Old Social Classes And The Revolutionary Movements Of Iraq*
Ha-Joon Chang's *Kicking Away the Ladder*
W. E. B. Du Bois's *The Souls of Black Folk*
Émile Durkheim's *On Suicide*
Frantz Fanon's *Black Skin, White Masks*
Frantz Fanon's *The Wretched of the Earth*
Eric Foner's *Reconstruction: America's Unfinished Revolution, 1863-1877*
Eugene Genovese's *Roll, Jordan, Roll: The World the Slaves Made*
Jack Goldstone's *Revolution and Rebellion in the Early Modern World*
Antonio Gramsci's *The Prison Notebooks*
Richard Herrnstein & Charles A Murray's *The Bell Curve: Intelligence and Class Structure in American Life*
Eric Hoffer's *The True Believer: Thoughts on the Nature of Mass Movements*
Jane Jacobs's *The Death and Life of Great American Cities*
Robert Lucas's *Why Doesn't Capital Flow from Rich to Poor Countries?*
Jay Macleod's *Ain't No Makin' It: Aspirations and Attainment in a Low Income Neighborhood*
Elaine May's *Homeward Bound: American Families in the Cold War Era*
Douglas McGregor's *The Human Side of Enterprise*
C. Wright Mills's *The Sociological Imagination*

Thomas Piketty's *Capital in the Twenty-First Century*
Robert D. Putman's *Bowling Alone*
David Riesman's *The Lonely Crowd: A Study of the Changing American Character*
Edward Said's *Orientalism*
Joan Wallach Scott's *Gender and the Politics of History*
Theda Skocpol's *States and Social Revolutions*
Max Weber's *The Protestant Ethic and the Spirit of Capitalism*

THEOLOGY

Augustine's *Confessions*
Benedict's *Rule of St Benedict*
Gustavo Gutiérrez's *A Theology of Liberation*
Carole Hillenbrand's *The Crusades: Islamic Perspectives*
David Hume's *Dialogues Concerning Natural Religion*
Immanuel Kant's *Religion within the Boundaries of Mere Reason*
Ernst Kantorowicz's *The King's Two Bodies: A Study in Medieval Political Theology*
Søren Kierkegaard's *The Sickness Unto Death*
C. S. Lewis's *The Abolition of Man*
Saba Mahmood's *The Politics of Piety: The Islamic Revival and the Feminist Subject*
Baruch Spinoza's *Ethics*
Keith Thomas's *Religion and the Decline of Magic*

COMING SOON

Chris Argyris's *The Individual and the Organisation*
Seyla Benhabib's *The Rights of Others*
Walter Benjamin's *The Work Of Art in the Age of Mechanical Reproduction*
John Berger's *Ways of Seeing*
Pierre Bourdieu's *Outline of a Theory of Practice*
Mary Douglas's *Purity and Danger*
Roland Dworkin's *Taking Rights Seriously*
James G. March's *Exploration and Exploitation in Organisational Learning*
Ikujiro Nonaka's *A Dynamic Theory of Organizational Knowledge Creation*
Griselda Pollock's *Vision and Difference*
Amartya Sen's *Inequality Re-Examined*
Susan Sontag's *On Photography*
Yasser Tabbaa's *The Transformation of Islamic Art*
Ludwig von Mises's *Theory of Money and Credit*

Macat Disciplines

Access the greatest ideas and thinkers across entire disciplines, including

Postcolonial Studies

Roland Barthes's *Mythologies*
Frantz Fanon's *Black Skin, White Masks*
Homi K. Bhabha's *The Location of Culture*
Gustavo Gutiérrez's *A Theology of Liberation*
Edward Said's *Orientalism*
Gayatri Chakravorty Spivak's *Can the Subaltern Speak?*

Macat analyses are available from all good bookshops and libraries.

Access hundreds of analyses through one, multimedia tool.

Join free for one month **library.macat.com**

Macat Disciplines

Access the greatest ideas and thinkers across entire disciplines, including

AFRICANA STUDIES

Chinua Achebe's *An Image of Africa: Racism in Conrad's Heart of Darkness*

W. E. B. Du Bois's *The Souls of Black Folk*

Zora Neale Hurston's *Characteristics of Negro Expression*

Martin Luther King Jr.'s *Why We Can't Wait*

Toni Morrison's *Playing in the Dark: Whiteness in the American Literary Imagination*

Macat analyses are available from all good bookshops and libraries.

Access hundreds of analyses through one, multimedia tool.
Join free for one month **library.macat.com**

Macat Disciplines

Access the greatest ideas and thinkers across entire disciplines, including

FEMINISM, GENDER AND QUEER STUDIES

Simone De Beauvoir's
The Second Sex

Michel Foucault's
History of Sexuality

Betty Friedan's
The Feminine Mystique

Saba Mahmood's
*The Politics of Piety:
The Islamic Revival and
the Feminist Subject*

Joan Wallach Scott's
*Gender and the
Politics of History*

Mary Wollstonecraft's
*A Vindication of the
Rights of Woman*

Virginia Woolf's
A Room of One's Own

Judith Butler's
Gender Trouble

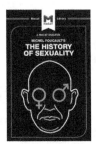

Macat analyses are available from all good bookshops and libraries.

Access hundreds of analyses through one, multimedia tool.
Join free for one month **library.macat.com**

Macat Disciplines

Access the greatest ideas and thinkers across entire disciplines, including

INEQUALITY

Ha-Joon Chang's, *Kicking Away the Ladder*

David Graeber's, *Debt: The First 5000 Years*

Robert E. Lucas's, *Why Doesn't Capital Flow from Rich To Poor Countries?*

Thomas Piketty's, *Capital in the Twenty-First Century*

Amartya Sen's, *Inequality Re-Examined*

Mahbub Ul Haq's, *Reflections on Human Development*

Macat analyses are available from all good bookshops and libraries.

Access hundreds of analyses through one, multimedia tool.
Join free for one month **library.macat.com**

Macat Disciplines

Access the greatest ideas and thinkers across entire disciplines, including

GLOBALIZATION

Arjun Appadurai's, *Modernity at Large: Cultural Dimensions of Globalisation*

James Ferguson's, *The Anti-Politics Machine*

Geert Hofstede's, *Culture's Consequences*

Amartya Sen's, *Development as Freedom*

Macat analyses are available from all good bookshops and libraries.

Access hundreds of analyses through one, multimedia tool.
Join free for one month **library.macat.com**

Macat Disciplines

Access the greatest ideas and thinkers across entire disciplines, including

MAN AND THE ENVIRONMENT

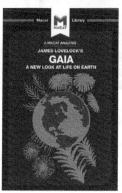
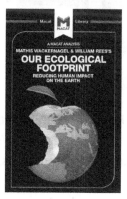

The Brundtland Report's, *Our Common Future*
Rachel Carson's, *Silent Spring*
James Lovelock's, *Gaia: A New Look at Life on Earth*
Mathis Wackernagel & William Rees's, *Our Ecological Footprint*

Macat analyses are available from all good bookshops and libraries.

Access hundreds of analyses through one, multimedia tool.
Join free for one month **library.macat.com**

Macat Disciplines

Access the greatest ideas and thinkers across entire disciplines, including

THE FUTURE OF DEMOCRACY

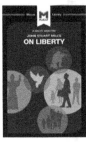   

Robert A. Dahl's, *Democracy and Its Critics*
Robert A. Dahl's, *Who Governs?*
Alexis De Toqueville's, *Democracy in America*
Niccolò Machiavelli's, *The Prince*
John Stuart Mill's, *On Liberty*
Robert D. Putnam's, *Bowling Alone*
Jean-Jacques Rousseau's, *The Social Contract*
Henry David Thoreau's, *Civil Disobedience*

Macat Pairs

Analyse historical and modern issues from opposite sides of an argument. Pairs include:

RACE AND IDENTITY

Zora Neale Hurston's
Characteristics of Negro Expression

Using material collected on anthropological expeditions to the South, Zora Neale Hurston explains how expression in African American culture in the early twentieth century departs from the art of white America. At the time, African American art was often criticized for copying white culture. For Hurston, this criticism misunderstood how art works. European tradition views art as something fixed. But Hurston describes a creative process that is alive, ever-changing, and largely improvisational. She maintains that African American art works through a process called 'mimicry'—where an imitated object or verbal pattern, for example, is reshaped and altered until it becomes something new, novel—and worthy of attention.

Frantz Fanon's
Black Skin, White Masks

Black Skin, White Masks offers a radical analysis of the psychological effects of colonization on the colonized.

Fanon witnessed the effects of colonization first hand both in his birthplace, Martinique, and again later in life when he worked as a psychiatrist in another French colony, Algeria. His text is uncompromising in form and argument. He dissects the dehumanizing effects of colonialism, arguing that it destroys the native sense of identity, forcing people to adapt to an alien set of values—including a core belief that they are inferior. This results in deep psychological trauma.

Fanon's work played a pivotal role in the civil rights movements of the 1960s.

Macat analyses are available from all good bookshops and libraries.

Access hundreds of analyses through one, multimedia tool.
Join free for one month **library.macat.com**

Macat Pairs

Analyse historical and modern issues from opposite sides of an argument. Pairs include:

INTERNATIONAL RELATIONS IN THE 21ST CENTURY

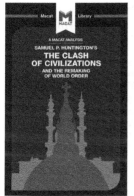

Samuel P. Huntington's
The Clash of Civilisations

In his highly influential 1996 book, Huntington offers a vision of a post-Cold War world in which conflict takes place not between competing ideologies but between cultures. The worst clash, he argues, will be between the Islamic world and the West: the West's arrogance and belief that its culture is a "gift" to the world will come into conflict with Islam's obstinacy and concern that its culture is under attack from a morally decadent "other."

Clash inspired much debate between different political schools of thought. But its greatest impact came in helping define American foreign policy in the wake of the 2001 terrorist attacks in New York and Washington.

Francis Fukuyama's
The End of History and the Last Man

Published in 1992, *The End of History and the Last Man* argues that capitalist democracy is the final destination for all societies. Fukuyama believed democracy triumphed during the Cold War because it lacks the "fundamental contradictions" inherent in communism and satisfies our yearning for freedom and equality. Democracy therefore marks the endpoint in the evolution of ideology, and so the "end of history." There will still be "events," but no fundamental change in ideology.

Macat analyses are available from all good bookshops and libraries.

Access hundreds of analyses through one, multimedia tool.
Join free for one month **library.macat.com**

Macat Pairs

Analyse historical and modern issues from opposite sides of an argument. Pairs include:

HOW TO RUN AN ECONOMY

John Maynard Keynes's
The General Theory OF Employment, Interest and Money

Classical economics suggests that market economies are self-correcting in times of recession or depression, and tend toward full employment and output. But English economist John Maynard Keynes disagrees.

In his ground-breaking 1936 study *The General Theory*, Keynes argues that traditional economics has misunderstood the causes of unemployment. Employment is not determined by the price of labor; it is directly linked to demand. Keynes believes market economies are by nature unstable, and so require government intervention. Spurred on by the social catastrophe of the Great Depression of the 1930s, he sets out to revolutionize the way the world thinks

Milton Friedman's
The Role of Monetary Policy

Friedman's 1968 paper changed the course of economic theory. In just 17 pages, he demolished existing theory and outlined an effective alternate monetary policy designed to secure 'high employment, stable prices and rapid growth.'

Friedman demonstrated that monetary policy plays a vital role in broader economic stability and argued that economists got their monetary policy wrong in the 1950s and 1960s by misunderstanding the relationship between inflation and unemployment. Previous generations of economists had believed that governments could permanently decrease unemployment by permitting inflation—and vice versa. Friedman's most original contribution was to show that this supposed trade-off is an illusion that only works in the short term.

Macat analyses are available from all good bookshops and libraries.

Access hundreds of analyses through one, multimedia tool.
Join free for one month **library.macat.com**

Macat Pairs

*Analyse historical and modern issues
from opposite sides of an argument.
Pairs include:*

HOW WE RELATE TO EACH OTHER AND SOCIETY

Jean-Jacques Rousseau's
The Social Contract

Rousseau's famous work sets out the radical concept of the 'social contract': a give-and-take relationship between individual freedom and social order.

If people are free to do as they like, governed only by their own sense of justice, they are also vulnerable to chaos and violence. To avoid this, Rousseau proposes, they should agree to give up some freedom to benefit from the protection of social and political organization. But this deal is only just if societies are led by the collective needs and desires of the people, and able to control the private interests of individuals. For Rousseau, the only legitimate form of government is rule by the people.

Robert D. Putnam's
Bowling Alone

In *Bowling Alone*, Robert Putnam argues that Americans have become disconnected from one another and from the institutions of their common life, and investigates the consequences of this change.

Looking at a range of indicators, from membership in formal organizations to the number of invitations being extended to informal dinner parties, Putnam demonstrates that Americans are interacting less and creating less "social capital" – with potentially disastrous implications for their society.

It would be difficult to overstate the impact of *Bowling Alone*, one of the most frequently cited social science publications of the last half-century.

Macat analyses are available from all good bookshops and libraries.

Access hundreds of analyses through one, multimedia tool.
Join free for one month **library.macat.com**

For Product Safety Concerns and Information please contact our EU
representative GPSR@taylorandfrancis.com Taylor & Francis Verlag GmbH,
Kaufingerstraße 24, 80331 München, Germany

Printed and bound by CPI Group (UK) Ltd, Croydon, CR0 4YY
08/06/2025
01896977-0004